The Daily Telegraph
Quick Crossword Book
34

Also available in Pan Books

The Daily Telegraph
Quick Crossword Book
34

Pan Books
in association with *The Daily Telegraph*

First published in 2003 by Pan Books

This edition first published 2018 by Pan Books
an imprint of Pan Macmillan
20 New Wharf Road, London N1 9RR
Associated companies throughout the world
www.panmacmillan.com

In association with *The Daily Telegraph*

ISBN 978-1-509-89389-8

Copyright © Telegraph Group Limited 2003

The right of *The Daily Telegraph* to be identified as the author of
this work has been asserted by it in accordance with the
Copyright, Designs and Patents Act 1988.

A CIP catalogue record for this book is available from the
British Library.

ACROSS

1 Run short (8)
7 Weapon shot by bow (5)
8 Recklessly bold (9)
9 Female member of religious order (3)
10 Naked truth (4)
11 Schedule of business (6)
13 Inexperienced (6)
14 Small breed of hound (6)
17 Beverage (6)
18 Complete failure (4)
20 Hint (3)
22 Storyteller (9)
23 Male duck (5)
24 Make known publicly (8)

DOWN

1 Rod, pole (5)
2 Basic (7)
3 Small isle (4)
4 Sufficient (6)
5 Combat area (5)
6 Peter out (7)
7 Apart (7)
12 Large outdoor conflagration (7)
13 Waterfall (7)
15 Large sailing ship (7)
16 Signal light on a hill (6)
17 Tree (5)
19 Boxer's prize (5)
21 —— Domini (4)

2

ACROSS

1 South-east Asian republic (7)
5 Dressed in (4)
7 Type of pastry (5)
8 Illness (6)
10 Whip (4)
11 Fearful (8)
13 Saudi capital (6)
14 The Twins (6)
17 Unsightliness (8)
19 Closed (4)
21 Total (6)
22 Non-rural (5)
23 Beseech (4)
24 Operating room (7)

DOWN

1 Noisy (10)
2 Frugality (7)
3 Following (4)
4 Biography (6)
5 Easy victory (4-4)
6 Wireless (5)
9 Avail (10)
12 Individuality (8)
15 Restrain (7)
16 Appearance (6)
18 Of the moon (5)
20 User (anag.) (4)

ACROSS

1 Rest from work (4)
4 Offers in payment (7)
8 Rescind (8)
9 Hill (3)
11 Direct (anag.) (6)
13 Graeco-Turkish sea (6)
14 Mob (5)
15 Sit or travel on (4)
17 Repast (4)
18 Brush clean (5)
20 Prevail on (6)
21 Philip ——, poet (6)
24 Poem (3)
25 Twining shoots (8)
26 Spanish wine-cup (7)
27 Final (4)

DOWN

2 An easy pace (5)
3 Alien, outlandish (6)
4 A hardwood (4)
5 Required (6)
6 Utmost limit (7)
7 Scattering drops (10)
10 Defamatory (10)
12 Moment (5)
13 Terrible (5)
16 Offended indignation (7)
18 Sea duck (6)
19 Tun (6)
22 *The Book of* —— (5)
23 People of Peru (4)

4

ACROSS

1 1st Channel swimmer (4)
4 Spectacles (6)
7 Vase (3)
9 Stupefy (4)
10 Theatre break (8)
11 Nap (3)
12 Faithful (4)
13 Runs seed (anag.) (3-5)
16 Transvestites (5-8)
19 Agreed (8)
23 —— Major (stars) (4)
24 Not on (3)
25 Nestles (8)
26 —— Trueman (sport) (4)
27 Old cloth measure (3)
28 Besought (6)
29 Simple (4)

DOWN

2 Adventurous (12)
3 Golfer's hazards (7)
4 Marsh bird (5)
5 Punished by curfew (5)
6 Aquatic birds (5)
8 Barbers (12)
14 eg Sister (5)
15 —— and downs (3)
17 eg Lust, Envy (3)
18 Mix the cards (7)
20 Keen (5)
21 Television (5)
22 Gave medicine (5)

ACROSS

1 Before long (4)
5 Land forces (4)
7 Entwined (7)
8 Woollens (8)
10 Wisecrack (4)
12 Aquatic bird (4)
14 US state (8)
16 Disloyalty (8)
17 Famous school (4)
18 Italian wine (4)
19 Channel Island (8)
22 Demonstrating (7)
23 Asian desert (4)
24 Seedcase (4)

DOWN

1 Channel Island (4)
2 Eft (4)
3 Channel Island (8)
4 Wound mark (4)
5 Sufficient (8)
6 March while laden (4)
9 Novelty (7)
11 Tedious (7)
13 Spring flowers (8)
15 News broadcast (8)
18 Keen (4)
19 Hired thug (4)
20 Near (4)
21 Jerk (4)

6

ACROSS

1 *Ex gratia* payment (5)
4 Nicks (7)
8 Texan city (7)
9 Bulky (5)
10 Robbery (5)
11 Ancestry (7)
13 Waterside plant (4)
15 Over there (6)
17 Consequence (6)
20 Heavenly body (4)
22 Large jug (7)
24 Scare (5)
26 Flask (5)
27 Type of ship (7)
28 Beneficiary (7)
29 Oust (5)

DOWN

1 Lay bets (anag.) (7)
2 Din (5)
3 Ghost (7)
4 Sewing implement (6)
5 Claw (5)
6 Grass (7)
7 Scandinavian (5)
12 Notion (4)
14 Gaelic (4)
16 Nought (7)
18 Delicate (7)
19 Storm (7)
21 A little; sweet (6)
22 Student (5)
23 *The Planets* composer (5)
25 Chalcedony gemstone (5)

ACROSS

1 Lure (4)
3 Region of Central France (8)
9 Constant, true (5)
10 Train of followers (7)
11 Request (3)
13 Bandit (9)
14 Happen (6)
16 Thwart, hinder (6)
18 Disturbance (9)
20 Mineral spring (3)
22 Accent, patois (7)
23 Trance (5)
25 Sauce for food (8)
26 Develop (4)

DOWN

1 Light wood (5)
2 Climbing plant (3)
4 Uneasy state (6)
5 Beg (7)
6 French policemen (9)
7 Ugly thing (7)
8 Pleased (4)
12 Oceanic gull (9)
14 Marked by heated iron (7)
15 Merchants (7)
17 Hark (6)
19 Cosy home (4)
21 Permit (5)
24 Attention (3)

ACROSS

1 Hewn stone (5)
4 Assisting (6)
9 Intricate (7)
10 Perception (5)
11 Reverberate (4)
12 Cut of beef (7)
13 Overweight (3)
14 Bucket (4)
16 Foundation; ignoble (4)
18 Prosecute (3)
20 Brass instrument (7)
21 Duelling-sword (4)
24 Raccoon-like animal (5)
25 Number (7)
26 Substitute (6)
27 Greek poet (5)

DOWN

1 Wrangle (6)
2 Sex appeal (5)
3 Hindu goddess (4)
5 Nice ribs (anag.) (8)
6 Fiery (7)
7 Graham ——— , novelist (6)
8 Live (5)
13 Frivolous (8)
15 Former student (7)
17 Paper-clip (6)
18 Smelt foul (5)
19 Underground room (6)
22 Jewish festival (5)
23 Eastern nursemaid (4)

ACROSS

1 More tranquil (6)
4 Illumination (5)
8 —— Tuck (5)
9 Retribution (7)
10 Close of day (7)
11 Nothing (4)
12 Droop (3)
14 Purposes (4)
15 Trick (4)
18 Part of foot (3)
21 & 23 TV impressionist (4,7)
25 Firedog (7)
26 Reproductive gland (5)
27 Tales (5)
28 Thicker (6)

DOWN

1 Beverage (6)
2 Lingers (7)
3 Soonest (8)
4 Charged with electricity (4)
5 Djinn (5)
6 Vibration (6)
7 Rocks, cliffs (5)
13 Grisly (8)
16 Open shoes (7)
17 Formal agreement (6)
19 Black wood (5)
20 Petition to God (6)
22 Corollary to a contract (5)
24 Poetry, music etc (4)

10

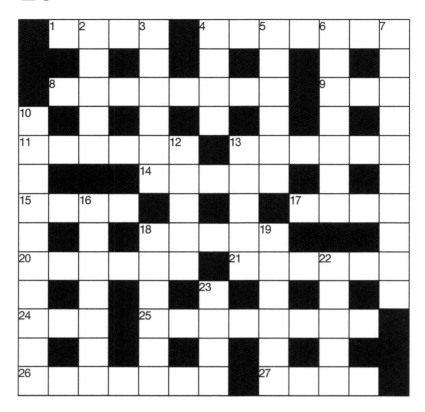

ACROSS

1 Bosun's whistle (4)
4 Sound of a sneeze (7)
8 Uninformed (8)
9 Joan of —— (3)
11 County in Ulster (6)
13 Locomotive (6)
14 God of love (5)
15 Dim (4)
17 Jog (4)
18 Isle of —— (5)
20 Polar region (6)
21 Frozen plain (6)
24 Neckwear (3)
25 Sceptic (8)
26 Remainder (7)
27 Otherwise (4)

DOWN

2 Gold bar (5)
3 Outlandish (6)
4 At a distance (4)
5 Plan (6)
6 Weightier (7)
7 Shore carts (anag.) (10)
10 Military conductor (10)
12 *The Sound of* —— (5)
13 Rowing team (5)
16 Footmen (7)
18 *The* —— *of Oz* (6)
19 Sharp struggle (6)
22 Evaporates (5)
23 At one time (4)

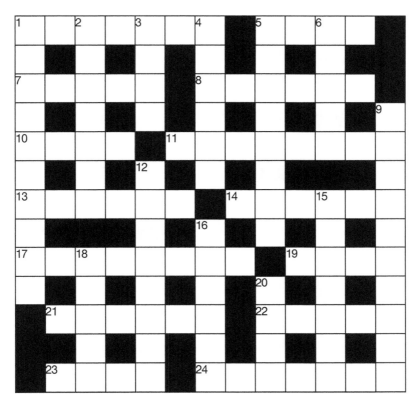

ACROSS

1 Room (7)
5 Narrow road (4)
7 Socialiser (5)
8 Broker (6)
10 Expedition (4)
11 Time (8)
13 Plan (6)
14 Eat hastily (6)
17 Female (8)
19 Proceed (4)
21 Busy (6)
22 Dust-coloured (5)
23 Crazy (4)
24 Brochure (7)

DOWN

1 Awaken (4,2,4)
2 Uneasiness (7)
3 Poet (4)
4 Refuse (6)
5 Larboard (anag.) (8)
6 Birthmarks (5)
9 Petticoat (10)
12 Amount (8)
15 Boring tool (7)
16 Imaginary (6)
18 Coffee (5)
20 Lady's fingers (4)

12

ACROSS

1 Ova (4)
3 The sound of "h" (8)
9 Name (5)
10 Set apart (7)
11 A bite; a drink (3)
13 Careless (9)
14 Middle (6)
16 Thought alike (6)
18 Bride's clothes (9)
20 Afternoon meal (3)
22 Dried fruit (7)
23 Faithful (5)
25 Canines (8)
26 Twist (4)

DOWN

1 Consumed (5)
2 Obtain (3)
4 Mean (6)
5 Pressing (7)
6 Mean beast (anag.) (9)
7 Chosen (7)
8 Blood-vessel (4)
12 Christmas show (9)
14 Exclusive clique (7)
15 Intermission (7)
17 Minimal accommodation (6)
19 Unsightly (4)
21 Permit (5)
24 Tibetan animal (3)

ACROSS

1 *Auld —— Syne* (4)
4 Expressing desire (7)
8 Contemptuous (8)
9 Beverage (3)
11 Painter (6)
13 Intense dislike (6)
14 Refuge (5)
15 Renown (4)
17 Leave out (4)
18 Cache (5)
20 Deep dish with cover (6)
21 Scottish clan design (6)
24 Small shed (3)
25 Spotted beetle (8)
26 Marine mammal (7)
27 Level, flat (4)

DOWN

2 Berkshire racecourse (5)
3 Gaudy (6)
4 Married woman (4)
5 Of woods or forests (6)
6 The meantime (7)
7 Terraced block of seats at sports events (10)
10 Unlikely (3-7)
12 Bird's hooked claw (5)
13 Core (5)
16 Relating to marriage (7)
18 Fitness (6)
19 Dip into, play at (6)
22 Neatly brief (5)
23 Place of great delight (4)

14

ACROSS

1 Jacket (6)
4 Track (5)
8 Dowdy woman (5)
9 Slope (7)
10 Tomb inscription (7)
11 Wild cat (4)
12 Greek "t" (3)
14 Fairy (4)
15 Bright star (4)
18 Diocese; look (3)
21 Good fortune (4)
23 Stealthy searcher (7)
25 Shambolic (7)
26 Damp (5)
27 Concede (5)
28 Houseman (6)

DOWN

1 Self-service meal (6)
2 Vituperative (7)
3 Stress (8)
4 Credit (4)
5 Farewell (5)
6 Room to manoeuvre (6)
7 Tipsy (5)
13 Rare (8)
16 Foxlike (7)
17 Courageous (6)
19 Era (5)
20 Nectar (anag.) (6)
22 Discontinue (5)
24 Breeding stallion (4)

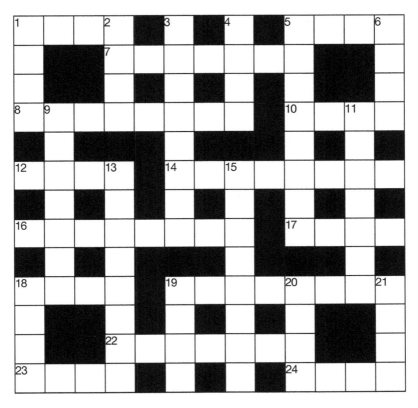

ACROSS

1 Pin, nail (4)
5 Roof or floor slab (4)
7 LA's ruin (anag.) (7)
8 Enmeshing (8)
10 Numerous (4)
12 Speech defect (4)
14 Abolished (8)
16 Feeling (8)
17 Valley (4)
18 Repast (4)
19 EC agricultural scheme (3-5)
22 Neonatal (7)
23 Orient (4)
24 Therefore (Latin) (4)

DOWN

1 Acidic; pastry (4)
2 Monarch (4)
3 Judge the worth (8)
4 Garden pest (4)
5 Quivered (8)
6 Facile (4)
9 Kansas cattle town (7)
11 Goaded, irritated (7)
13 Peevish, capricious (8)
15 To anoint (anag.) (8)
18 Pool (4)
19 Stitched (4)
20 Rational (4)
21 Reflected sound (4)

16

ACROSS

1 £1000 (sl.) (5)
4 p. (mus.) (5)
10 He argues formally (7)
11 —— *Laurie* (song) (5)
12 Vertical pipe (5)
13 Curtail (7)
15 Church recess (4)
17 Unmoving (5)
19 Waterway (5)
22 Employer (4)
25 Stinted (anag.) (7)
27 Viper (5)
29 Lively (5)
30 Mimic (7)
31 Tale (5)
32 Ire (5)

DOWN

2 Puzzle (5)
3 Unaffected (7)
5 US state (5)
6 *No, No,* —— (musical) (7)
7 Worship (5)
8 144 (5)
9 p. (coin) (5)
14 In this place (4)
16 + (4)
18 Smallest (7)
20 eg From Teheran (7)
21 Perfect (5)
23 Undress (5)
24 Gluttony (5)
26 Milan team; bury (5)
28 Male duck (5)

ACROSS

1 Visiting stores (8)
5 Handle clumsily (4)
8 Statuette (8)
9 Light fawn (4)
11 Trio (11)
14 Drag heavily (3)
16 Fibbing (5)
17 Rug (3)
18 Flourishing (5,6)
21 Burial-vault (4)
22 Hot-tempered person (8)
24 Dismal (4)
25 Man appointed by testator (8)

DOWN

1 Cushioned (4)
2 Should (5)
3 Banter (10)
4 Absence of (prefix) (3)
6 Hail (7)
7 Poet —— (8)
10 Giant disco (anag.) (10)
12 Damp (5)
13 Insulted (8)
15 Gleam (7)
19 Culpability (5)
20 Mock (4)
23 Peace (3)

18

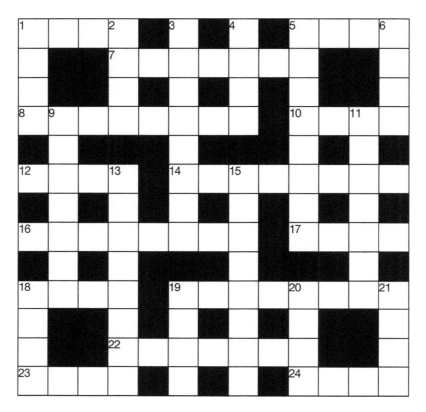

ACROSS

1 Golfer's warning (4)
5 Chinese dynasty (4)
7 Refuse (7)
8 Drive lob (anag.) (8)
10 Centre (4)
12 Leap (4)
14 Ingress (8)
16 Arbitrator (8)
17 Authentic (4)
18 Agitate (4)
19 Boughs (8)
22 Assistance (7)
23 Harbour; spy (4)
24 Wicked (4)

DOWN

1 Dolt (4)
2 Rim (4)
3 Mishap (8)
4 Untamed (4)
5 Trader (8)
6 Donate (4)
9 Wealthy (7)
11 Hermit (7)
13 Spring flower (8)
15 Culinary herb (8)
18 Stalk (4)
19 Rear (4)
20 Concern (4)
21 Vend (4)

ACROSS

1 More cunning (7)
5 Sordid (5)
8 Asserts (5)
9 Caribbean island (7)
10 Driving mechanism (9)
12 Noise (3)
13 Messy (6)
14 Inclined (6)
17 Wildebeest (3)
18 Rest (9)
20 Clasp (7)
21 Greek order (5)
23 Lamp (5)
24 Girl's name (7)

DOWN

1 Muscular affliction (5)
2 Born (3)
3 In place (of) (7)
4 Entertain, feast (6)
5 Direct (5)
6 Left (9)
7 Longed (7)
11 Be more numerous than (9)
13 Ointment (7)
15 Issue (7)
16 Protozoon (6)
18 Attain (5)
19 Frill (5)
22 eg Almond (3)

20

ACROSS

1 Roof projections (5)
4 Dessert (7)
8 Unfortunate (7)
9 Behest; arrangement (5)
10 Debar (anag.) (5)
11 Threatening (7)
13 *Old Testament* book (4)
15 Tone-colour (6)
17 Hot spring (6)
20 Assault (4)
22 Huge number (7)
24 Kashmiri river (5)
26 Cake topping (5)
27 Free time (7)
28 Brought to bear (7)
29 Laud (5)

DOWN

1 Display (7)
2 Adder (5)
3 Slim (7)
4 Minister (6)
5 Loincloth (5)
6 In the house (7)
7 Hindu teachers (5)
12 Wise men (4)
14 Nought (4)
16 Mild sickness (7)
18 Building (7)
19 Bertrand ——,
philosopher (7)
21 Fished (6)
22 Formerly the Congo (5)
23 Metal bar (5)
25 Uncertainty (5)

ACROSS

1 Profound (4)
5 Wiles (4)
7 Sceptre (anag.) (7)
8 Street-light (4-4)
10 Dutch cheese (4)
12 Cook (4)
14 Provoke (8)
16 Separated (8)
17 Dreadful (4)
18 Finest (4)
19 Finish (8)
22 Antagonist (7)
23 Ripped (4)
24 Deadly sin (4)

DOWN

1 Timber; trade (4)
2 Support (4)
3 Amaze (8)
4 Tidy (4)
5 Gave evidence (8)
6 Appear (4)
9 Accomplish (7)
11 Changed (7)
13 Portion (8)
15 Incivility (8)
18 Footwear (4)
19 Manage (4)
20 Attraction (4)
21 Simple (4)

22

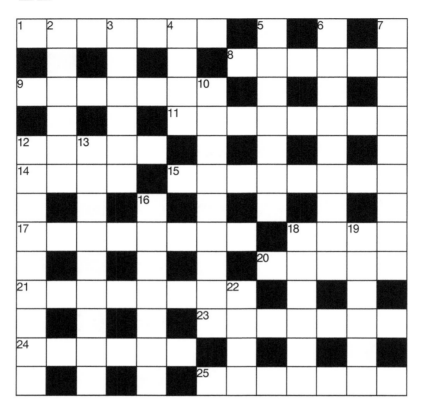

ACROSS

1 Chamber of —— (7)
8 Conservatives (6)
9 Wagering (7)
11 Brass instrument (8)
12 Cowboy show (5)
14 Soon (4)
15 Steed & Emma Peel (TV) (8)
17 Everlasting duration (8)
18 Principal character (4)
20 Screen again (5)
21 Defensive mounds (8)
23 Otic pain (7)
24 Wax cylinder (6)
25 Hip side (anag.) (7)

DOWN

2 Fairy king (6)
3 Putrefied (6)
4 Small pig (4)
5 Harass (7)
6 Kitchen tool (3-6)
7 A son's nice (anag.) (9)
10 Tend towards earth (9)
12 eg Epsom (9)
13 German guard dogs (9)
16 Effeminate (7)
18 Proclaim (6)
19 Stampedes (6)
22 Female Hindu garment (4)

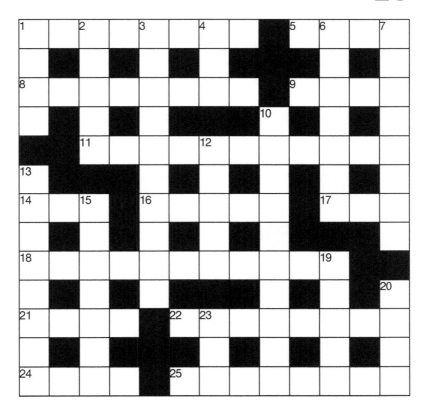

ACROSS

1 Kerosene (8)
5 *Inter* —— (among other things) (4)
8 Hurting (8)
9 Matured (4)
11 Take temporary charge (4,3,4)
14 Summit; child's toy (3)
16 Freshwater fish (5)
17 Low (3)
18 Striking (3-8)
21 Touch gently (4)
22 Inconstant (8)
24 Impolite (4)
25 UK mountain chain (8)

DOWN

1 Agony (4)
2 Indian prince (5)
3 Nevertheless (3,3,4)
4 Pub (3)
6 Space in a car (7)
7 Summation (8)
10 Laboratory worker (10)
12 Pick-me-up (5)
13 Naked runner (8)
15 Elapsed (anag.) (7)
19 It's capital city is Libreville (5)
20 Chief Greek god (4)
23 Beer (3)

24

ACROSS

1 Spiteful (5)
4 Columns (7)
8 Biting (7)
9 Go bad (5)
10 Vegetable (5)
11 Repeat (7)
13 Whirlpool (4)
15 Diatribe (6)
17 Even-tempered (6)
20 Unencumbered (4)
22 Rejoinder (7)
24 Blacksmith's tool (5)
26 Severe (5)
27 Can shut (anag.) (7)
28 Illicit liquor-shop (7)
29 German industrial city (5)

DOWN

1 Relief (7)
2 Ankle bones (5)
3 Longed (7)
4 Rotten (6)
5 Soup-server (5)
6 Very old (7)
7 Fashion (5)
12 Sort (4)
14 Dextrous (4)
16 Euphoria (7)
18 Foliage (7)
19 Marine mammal (7)
21 Argue (6)
22 Peruses (5)
23 Vegetable (5)
25 Goddess of love (5)

ACROSS

1 Contribute, begin energetically (5,2)
5 Complete (5)
8 Not appropriate (5)
9 Woollen closely-twisted yarn (7)
10 Young child (7)
11 Esoteric, private (5)
12 Latitude (6)
14 Small sturdy hound (6)
17 Lowest point (5)
19 Widely admired (7)
22 Apathy (7)
23 Once more (5)
24 Christened (5)
25 Major area of military activity (7)

DOWN

1 Pigment (5)
2 Balderdash (7)
3 Inn (5)
4 City in New Jersey (6)
5 Hostile (7)
6 Frequently (5)
7 Authorise, back (7)
12 Oil extracted from sheep's wool (7)
13 Beached (7)
15 Brave and honourable (7)
16 Essence, mettle (6)
18 Hard-wearing twill (5)
20 Location (5)
21 Wash lightly without soap (5)

26

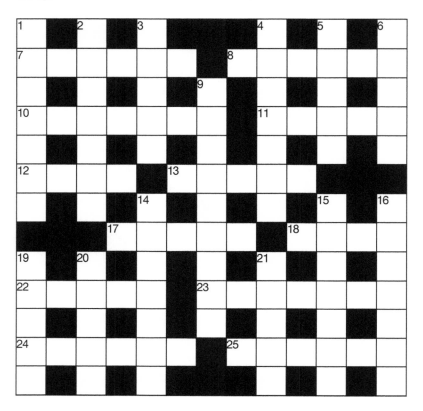

ACROSS

7 Restaurant server (6)
8 Tiny (6)
10 Byword (7)
11 Register (5)
12 Large pitcher (4)
13 Lifting tackle (5)
17 Flinch; game-bird (5)
18 Musical ending (4)
22 Triple-time dance (5)
23 Sheep's disease (7)
24 Watch; esteem (6)
25 University exams (6)

DOWN

1 Exchanged (7)
2 Prejudiced (7)
3 Gem (5)
4 Subtlety (7)
5 Foible (5)
6 Beautiful woman (5)
9 Of the belly (9)
14 Bird of prey (7)
15 Magazine (7)
16 Communist (7)
19 Cluster of bees (5)
20 Plaintive poem (5)
21 Saint (anag.) (5)

ACROSS

1 Rough and husky (6)
4 Copper-zinc alloy (5)
8 Get up (5)
9 Type of beer (7)
10 Avoidance, excuse (7)
11 Wheel pivot (4)
12 Bind (3)
14 Humped ox (4)
15 Rontgen's diagnostic aid (1-3)
18 Appeal for help (3)
21 Finished (4)
23 Advance showing (7)
25 Bulky, huge (7)
26 Male honey-bee (5)
27 Blood-sucker (5)
28 Farewells (6)

DOWN

1 Paradise (6)
2 Living (7)
3 Plausible but wrong (8)
4 Audacious (4)
5 Append, attach (5)
6 Water-ice (6)
7 Exhausted (5)
13 Lengthened (8)
16 Fatty (7)
17 Ceremonious (6)
19 Glib line of talk (5)
20 Confectionery (6)
22 Follow (5)
24 —— -helmet, or sola topi (4)

28

ACROSS

1 Located (7)
5 Little Richard (4)
7 W H ——— (poet) (5)
8 Car instrument-board (6)
10 Den (4)
11 Wood hyacinth (8)
13 Outcome (6)
14 Fisherman (6)
17 Coffee machine (8)
19 Chant (4)
21 Red gut (anag.) (6)
22 Weigh with lead (5)
23 Defect (4)
24 Hide (7)

DOWN

1 Oliver Hardy's partner (4,6)
2 Decrees (7)
3 Geordie river (4)
4 Gorge (6)
5 Makes out (8)
6 Offence (5)
9 Rhett in *Gone with the Wind* (5,5)
12 Melon variety (8)
15 Free-time (7)
16 Estimate (6)
18 Danger (5)
20 eg *Iliad* (4)

ACROSS

1 Kick (4)
5 Hardwood (4)
7 Insulting (7)
8 Enthusiasm (8)
10 Scrum (4)
12 Quick (4)
14 Snowstorm (8)
16 Share of profits (8)
17 Milky gem (4)
18 Yank (4)
19 Motionless (8)
22 Article (anag.) (7)
23 Small horse (4)
24 Defrost (4)

DOWN

1 Yap (4)
2 Mountain lake (4)
3 Fertile female insect (5,3)
4 One-sidedness (4)
5 Mosaic covering (8)
6 Scottish church (4)
9 Inspect (7)
11 Slaughter (7)
13 Artifice (8)
15 Point out (8)
18 Leap (4)
19 Stream (4)
20 Movement of a tune (4)
21 Attraction (4)

30

ACROSS

1 Ova (4)
4 Instructed (6)
7 Atmosphere (3)
9 Post (4)
10 Adroitly (anag.) (8)
11 Contend (3)
12 Notion (4)
13 Hollander (8)
16 Denial of the spiritual (13)
19 Agreed (8)
23 Panache (4)
24 Unit (3)
25 Acrimoniously (8)
26 Downpour (4)
27 Female sheep (3)
28 Out of sight (6)
29 Sand-hill (4)

DOWN

2 Protection (12)
3 Save (7)
4 Attempted (5)
5 German submarine (1-4)
6 Moor (5)
8 System, group (12)
14 Custom (5)
15 Greek letter (3)
17 Flee (3)
18 Guided (7)
20 Consumed (5)
21 Curt (5)
22 Senior member (5)

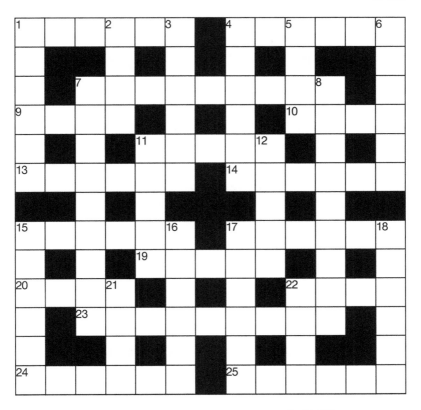

ACROSS

1 Alluring sea-nymphs (6)
4 Biblical queen (6)
7 Blockhead (9)
9 Radicle (4)
10 Swelling (4)
11 Mountain range (5)
13 Card game (6)
14 Those tending the sick (6)
15 Deliverance (6)
17 Opera by Bizet (6)
19 Mistake (5)
20 Location (4)
22 Uneven walk (4)
23 Having keen sight (5-4)
24 High-quality grape brandy (6)
25 Head-dress (6)

DOWN

1 Beetle (6)
2 Send forth (4)
3 Recumbent, flat (6)
4 Cricket team (6)
5 Implement (4)
6 Noisy commotion (6)
7 One prominent in fashionable society (9)
8 Nanny (9)
11 Consent (5)
12 Sucrose (5)
15 Bucolic (6)
16 Caper (6)
17 Clandestine (6)
18 Serviette (6)
21 Gain by labour (4)
22 Suggestive look (4)

32

ACROSS

1 Damsel (4)
3 Headway (8)
9 Vault (5)
10 Sailing boat (7)
11 Pale (3)
13 Flirtation (9)
14 Outcast (6)
16 Self-centred person (6)
18 End of chess game (9)
20 Epoch (3)
22 Tin-glazed earthenware (7)
23 Rushes; hides (5)
25 Australian capital (8)
26 Opposed to (4)

DOWN

1 Tropical parrot (5)
2 Hedera (3)
4 Remember (6)
5 Winning (7)
6 Costly (9)
7 Repents (anag.) (7)
8 Boss (4)
12 Scandinavian (9)
14 Peaceful (7)
15 Sideways (7)
17 Profession (6)
19 Exhibition (4)
21 Fire-raising (5)
24 Fell timber (3)

ACROSS

1 East Sussex town (5)
4 Christmas song (5)
10 Joking (7)
11 Raising agent (5)
12 Soup spoon (5)
13 Infuse gradually (7)
15 Not any (4)
17 Verity (5)
19 Expiate (5)
22 Mud (4)
25 Naval sword (7)
27 Radar beacon (5)
29 Spare (anag.) (5)
30 Distinguished (7)
31 —— Cavell, WWI nurse (5)
32 Man-made fibre (5)

DOWN

2 Finished (5)
3 Patent (7)
5 Bottomless chasm (5)
6 Round of applause (7)
7 Accomplishment (5)
8 Once more (5)
9 Not fresh (5)
14 Close by (4)
16 Units of electrical resistance (4)
18 Withdrawn (7)
20 Frighten (7)
21 Range (5)
23 Stile (anag.) (5)
24 Combine (5)
26 Representative (5)
28 Set of beliefs (5)

34

ACROSS

1 Sussex resort (4)
4 Enlightenment (7)
8 1's neighbour (8)
9 Forbid (3)
11 To the rear (6)
13 Hilaire —— (writer) (6)
14 Keen (5)
15 Indifferent (2-2)
17 Annul (4)
18 Songs for one (5)
20 Fruitlessly (2,4)
21 Just supposing ...? (4,2)
24 Anger (3)
25 *Nicholas* —— (Dickens) (8)
26 Ten less (anag.) (7)
27 Declares (4)

DOWN

2 —— Winfrey (TV) (5)
3 Locomotive (6)
4 Jot (4)
5 eg Canary (6)
6 French tapestry (7)
7 Musical notation system (5,3-2)
10 Ethiopian (10)
12 —— Runyon (writer) (5)
13 Under (5)
16 USSR Councils (7)
18 Gin, Sal ? (anag.) (6)
19 Pods (6)
22 Brindled cat (5)
23 Performs (4)

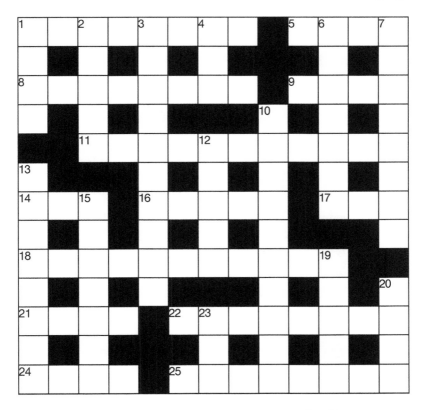

ACROSS

1 Undergarment (8)
5 To listen to (4)
8 Diplomatic mission (8)
9 To-do (4)
11 Business deal (11)
14 Tatter (3)
16 Armed (anag.) (5)
17 Firearm (3)
18 Plight (11)
21 Debauchee (4)
22 Scrawl (8)
24 Scandinavian (4)
25 Motionless (8)

DOWN

1 Scottish skirt (4)
2 Bar of gold (5)
3 Friends and relatives (4,3,3)
4 Marsupial (colloq.) (3)
6 Oozing out (7)
7 Resounding (8)
10 Running about briskly (10)
12 Ancient name of Yemen (5)
13 Ready (8)
15 Small cucumber (7)
19 Shinbone (5)
20 Outlet (4)
23 Carve (3)

36

ACROSS

1 Scrawny (4)
5 Monarch (4)
7 Viewpoint (7)
8 Elastic (8)
10 Coop (4)
12 Self-satisfied (4)
14 Precious metal (8)
16 Most stringent (8)
17 Sport (4)
18 Knock out (4)
19 Joins (8)
22 Raise (7)
23 Depend (4)
24 Require (4)

DOWN

1 Fling (4)
2 Short letter (4)
3 Follower (8)
4 Wee (4)
5 Rapping (8)
6 Stare (4)
9 Storm (7)
11 Gastronome (7)
13 Channel Island (8)
15 Feelers (8)
18 Dispute (4)
19 Cook (4)
20 Regular (4)
21 Rushed (4)

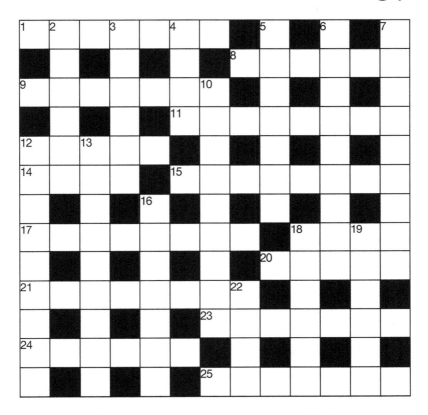

ACROSS

1 Nautical knot (7)
8 Ship's kitchen (6)
9 Sneakiness (7)
11 Dregs (8)
12 Devoutness (5)
14 Untie, ruin (4)
15 Asian legume (4,4)
17 Mixed drink (8)
18 Surrender (4)
20 Fault (5)
21 Melancholy (7)
21 Drug to counteract effects of poison (8)
24 He runs away to wed (6)
25 Branch of mathematics using symbols (7)

DOWN

2 Acquire (6)
3 Shed adjoining a wall (4-2)
4 Small gingery biscuits (4)
5 Natural home (7)
6 Signal flag of vessel about to sail (4,5)
7 Onlooker (9)
10 Pleasure seekers (9)
12 Buyer (9)
13 Schooling (9)
16 Academic work (7)
18 Cower, flinch (6)
19 Water-diviner (6)
22 Nobleman (4)

38

ACROSS

1 Casseroled (7)
5 Secret revelations (5)
8 Topic (anag.) (5)
9 Pasta dish (7)
10 Impetuous (9)
12 Grease (3)
13 Tropical fruit (6)
14 Slave to a habit (6)
17 Din; dispute (3)
18 Stuffing (9)
20 Greek "o" (7)
21 Fable writer (5)
23 Perspire (5)
24 Commanded (7)

DOWN

1 Thin soup (5)
2 Law (3)
3 Club (7)
4 Mock (6)
5 Furious (5)
6 Beg pardon (9)
7 Frying pan (7)
11 Use a keyboard (9)
13 Perilous (7)
15 Intransigent (3-4)
16 Spanish dictator (6)
18 Initial (5)
19 Lukewarm (5)
22 Baronet's title (3)

ACROSS

1 Boer defensive encampment (6)
4 Boors, oafs (5)
8 Garden flower (5)
9 Gauge (7)
10 African state (7)
11 Cow-barn (4)
12 Cut off top (3)
14 Profit (4)
15 Arguments (4)
18 Indian state (3)
21 Swedish pop group (4)
23 Wilts town (7)
25 Rider's foot-rest (7)
26 Small weight (5)
27 Dairy product (5)
28 Daises (anag.) (6)

DOWN

1 Be in touch (6)
2 Aerial, feeler (7)
3 Infuriating (8)
4 Fibber (4)
5 Illegal money lending (5)
6 Israeli monetary unit (6)
7 Diminutive (5)
13 Earlier, former (8)
16 Shrivelled, wrinkled (7)
17 Measurement unit for stellar distances (6)
19 Skilful (5)
20 Conducts, shows (6)
22 Newly-wed (5)
24 Neat, slim (4)

40

ACROSS

1 Long-term prisoner (5)
4 Inner Hebridean island (5)
10 Attire (7)
11 Parcel out (5)
12 Untrue (5)
13 High-speed road in the US (7)
15 Secure (4)
17 Trifling (5)
19 Examine (5)
22 Euro Free Trade Area (4)
25 Look down on (7)
27 Absolutely not! (2,3)
28 Nasal tone (5)
30 House on wheels (7)
31 Glamorgan town (5)
32 Portents (5)

DOWN

2 Urge forward (5)
3 *The Importance of Being —— (7)*
5 Frighten (5)
6 We all do (anag.) (7)
7 Blunder (5)
8 —— Richard (singer) (5)
9 Remains (5)
14 Repose (4)
16 The —— have it (4)
18 Subject (7)
20 Fit of temper (7)
21 Revises (5)
23 Barrier (5)
24 Laughing carnivore (5)
26 Gold bar (5)
28 Interlaced (5)

ACROSS

1 Dormant (8)
7 Spoil, prize (5)
8 Light racing boat (9)
9 Age (3)
10 Mere (4)
11 Nearer (6)
13 Cigarette (sl.) (6)
14 Inclines (6)
17 Gun dog (6)
18 Crystalline frozen vapour (4)
20 Swallow (3)
22 Biblical sea-monster (9)
23 Slack (5)
24 Keep safe (8)

DOWN

1 Lower oneself, bend (5)
2 Stretches out (7)
3 Demure, proper (4)
4 Worry, nag (6)
5 Wanderer (5)
6 Despots (7)
7 Short, stiff hair (7)
12 Fabric (7)
13 Spectral (7)
15 Black cat (7)
16 Colorado state capital (6)
17 Reel (5)
19 Flinch (5)
21 Girl (4)

42

ACROSS

1 Back lane (5)
2 —— of Seville (opera) (6)
9 Shrieks (7)
10 Hobo (5)
11 Fizzy drink (4)
12 US state (7)
13 Convulsion (3)
14 eg Wight (4)
16 Holier than —— (4)
18 Mineral (3)
20 Makes fizzy (7)
21 Mediterranean isle (4)
24 Spiced dish of rice (5)
25 Eluded (7)
26 Tried (6)
27 Verdant (5)

DOWN

1 Help (6)
2 Ghastly (5)
3 Twelve months (4)
5 I don't eat (anag.) (8)
6 Swagger (7)
7 Say again (6)
8 Savoury jelly (5)
13 Piece of laboratory equipment (4-4)
15 Saunters (7)
17 Floor covering (6)
18 Film award (5)
19 Guard (6)
22 Shelf (5)
23 Yearn (4)

ACROSS

1 Antelopes (4)
4 Press (6)
7 Increase (3)
9 Idiot (4)
10 Went up (8)
11 Distant (3)
12 Festivity (4)
13 Meal (8)
16 About (13)
19 Laughed (8)
23 Span (4)
24 Uncooked (3)
25 Leaflet (8)
26 Den (4)
27 Chopper (3)
28 Solicitor (6)
29 Crossbar (4)

DOWN

2 US state (3,9)
3 Expected to remain fine (3,4)
4 Paler (anag.) (5)
5 Hickory nut (5)
6 US farm (5)
8 Remembrance (12)
14 Amalgamate (5)
15 Tea (3)
17 Acorn tree (3)
18 Fishing-boat (7)
20 Hot drink (5)
21 Infested with lice (5)
22 Gloomy (5)

44

ACROSS

1 Breed of dog (6)
4 Avoids (5)
8 Memorise (5)
9 Yokel (7)
10 General (anag.) (7)
11 Back (4)
12 Owing (3)
14 Astound (4)
15 Common sense (4)
18 Plaything (3)
21 Weighty book (4)
23 Applause (7)
25 Doctor's client (7)
26 Semblance (5)
27 Funereal music (5)
28 Keen (6)

DOWN

1 Named (6)
2 Pamphlet (7)
3 Unaware (8)
4 Remain (4)
5 Custom (5)
6 Ringed planet (6)
7 Velocity (5)
13 Imperil (8)
16 Employ (7)
17 Vacuous (6)
19 Lad (5)
20 Disquiet (6)
22 Engine (5)
24 Lake (4)

ACROSS

1 Collier (5)
4 Net gains (7)
8 Side by side (7)
9 Check, dissuade (5)
10 Resided (5)
11 Boat crew (7)
13 Artists' paints (4)
15 Disc (6)
17 Disarrange (6)
20 Long narrative poem (4)
22 Care for, nurture (7)
24 Capsize (5)
26 Vigorous (5)
27 Gastronome (7)
28 Lightest known metal (7)
29 Leaflet (5)

DOWN

1 Follow winding course (7)
2 Tend, look after (5)
3 Device used to produce nuclear energy (7)
4 Gasoline (6)
5 Command (5)
6 Narrow strip of land (7)
7 Temptress (5)
12 Italian wine (4)
14 eg 15th March (4)
16 Pharmacist (7)
18 Ophthalmologist (7)
19 Beseech (7)
21 Apathy (6)
22 Swimming stroke (5)
23 Boadicea's tribe (5)
25 Finnish bath (5)

46

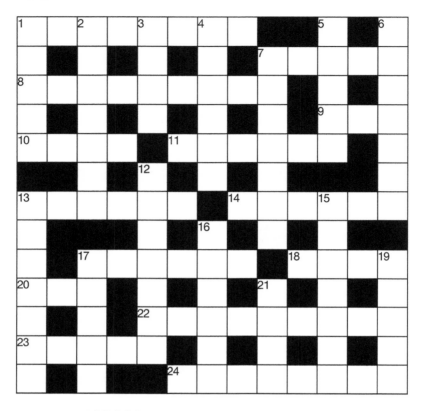

ACROSS

1 Bedcovers (8)
7 Tiny person (5)
8 Hospital vehicle (9)
9 Massage (3)
10 Cupola (4)
11 Lebanese capital (6)
13 eg Mushroom (6)
14 Light lunch (6)
17 Moroccan port (6)
18 Opposed to (4)
20 Illuminated (3)
22 Roman soldier (9)
23 Peal (5)
24 Tree-dwelling (8)

DOWN

1 Insipid (5)
2 Blame UN (anag.) (7)
3 Slaughter (4)
4 Sensitive (6)
5 Commence (5)
6 Illicit liquor shop (7)
7 Ground (7)
12 Long-lasting (7)
13 Misleading notion (7)
15 Military flourish (7)
16 Hang about (6)
17 Garret; Athenian (5)
19 Pastoral poem (5)
21 American tramp (4)

ACROSS

1 Parrot's name (5)
4 Italian painter (6)
9 Normal (7)
10 Sum (5)
11 Charged particles (4)
12 Flightless bird (7)
13 Underworld (3)
14 Ballet skirt (4)
16 Smooth (4)
18 Purpose (3)
20 I, so numb (anag) (7)
21 Church recess (4)
24 Eagle's nest (5)
25 Feat (7)
26 Magical incantations (6)
27 Loop; snare (5)

DOWN

1 Writing tool (6)
2 Classical language (5)
3 Three feet (4)
5 Together; one behind the other (2,6)
6 Butt in (7)
7 & 17 Willy-nilly (6,6)
8 Smacks (5)
13 Gym weight; idiot (sl.) (4-4)
15 Disconcert (7)
17 See 7
18 Michaelmas daisy (5)
19 In fine —— (6)
22 Snap (5)
23 Rotate (4)

48

ACROSS

1 Spirit of the lamp (5)
4 Hypersensitivity (7)
8 Pantomime hero (7)
9 Film (5)
10 Step (5)
11 Guaranteed (7)
13 Duelling sword (4)
15 Showy (6)
17 Beliefs (6)
20 Garden tool (4)
22 Cupboard (7)
24 Elector (5)
26 Imitating (5)
27 —— Gish (actress) (7)
28 Letters (anag.) (7)
29 Sloughs off; huts (5)

DOWN

1 Turfed (7)
2 Central African lake (5)
3 Undergoes (7)
4 BBC (sl.) (6)
5 Young sheep (5)
6 Invert (7)
7 Give in (5)
12 Impudence (sl.) (4)
14 Combustible pile (4)
16 Bed bite (anag.) (7)
18 Rebels (7)
19 Leaps (7)
21 Clement —— (PM) (6)
22 Sea map (5)
23 Darkness (5)
25 Petty (5)

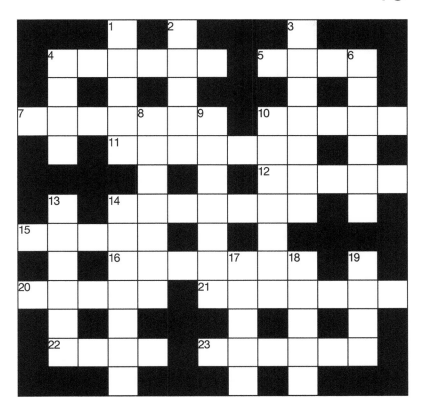

ACROSS

4 Gatherer (6)
5 Portal (4)
7 Reception room (7)
10 Exaggerated (5)
11 Measuring tube (7)
12 Means of access (5)
14 Guaranteed (7)
15 Mischievous trick (5)
16 Waistbelts (7)
20 Rents (anag.) (5)
21 Prime beef cut (7)
22 Young horse (4)
23 Red wine (6)

DOWN

1 Trophy of victory (5)
2 Establish (3,2)
3 Presage (7)
4 Chime (4)
6 Look at (6)
8 Waterproof cloth (7)
9 Repayments (7)
10 More exorbitant (7)
13 Carnal (6)
14 Crossly (7)
17 Cotton yarn (5)
18 Drink noisily (5)
19 Sieve (4)

50

ACROSS

1 Alien (7)
5 Unwell (4)
7 Sound entertainment (5)
8 Units of heat (6)
10 Dutch cheese (4)
11 Written agreement (8)
13 Forty winks (6)
14 Ten years (6)
17 Scrape it (anag.) (8)
19 Loud noise (4)
21 Look through (6)
22 Shatter (5)
23 Revered figure (4)
24 Inscribed (7)

DOWN

1 Safety device (4,6)
2 Beaming (7)
3 Press (4)
4 Idea (6)
5 Apparitions (8)
6 Punctuation mark (5)
9 Reinforce (10)
12 Bucolic (8)
15 Intransigent (7)
16 Avoid (6)
18 In front (5)
20 Sparkling wine (4)

ACROSS

1 Seemly, fitting (6)
2 Restricting student to college grounds (6)
7 Repugnant (9)
9 Flightless birds (4)
10 Sea-eagle (4)
11 Brute (5)
13 Declares (6)
14 Full bloom (6)
15 Strangers (6)
17 Indifference (6)
19 Long-legged wader (5)
20 Closed (4)
22 Sport for horse riders (4)
23 Sexton (9)
24 Savour, taste (6)
25 RAF personnel (6)

DOWN

1 Gripping tool (6)
2 Inns (4)
3 Greek island (6)
4 Gaudy (6)
5 Melody (4)
6 Jollity (6)
7 Recklessly daring (9)
8 Convention, folklore (9)
11 Pulse vegetables (5)
12 Allure (5)
15 Respond (6)
16 Stiffener (6)
17 US state (6)
18 eg Beefeater (6)
21 Cab (4)
22 Couple (4)

52

ACROSS

1 Lucas (anag.) (5)
4 Onward (5)
10 Under-bodice (7)
11 In slow tempo (5)
12 Loaded (5)
13 Prisoner (7)
15 Cicatrice (4)
17 Small character part (5)
19 North-west US state (5)
22 Extinct bird (4)
25 Mooring rope (7)
27 Sedate (5)
29 Italian explorer (5)
30 Imbecilic (7)
31 Round cap (5)
32 Brisk; brittle (5)

DOWN

2 Correct (5)
3 Authorise (7)
5 Kind of primula (5)
6 Taint (7)
7 Song of praise (5)
8 Heather (5)
9 Witches' meeting (5)
14 Dry (4)
16 Cipher (4)
18 Friendly (7)
20 File (7)
21 Room (5)
23 eg Kidney (5)
24 Bottle for condiments (5)
26 Denomination (5)
28 Ecstasy; composer (5)

ACROSS

1 Errand, vocation (7)
5 The Ram constellation (5)
8 Civil servants' union (5)
9 —— da Cunha (7)
10 Haven (7)
11 Bracing air (5)
12 Gap in defences (6)
14 Niche, alcove (6)
17 Siren (anag.) (5)
19 Rainy (7)
22 Former French colony (7)
23 Deal with (5)
24 —— Flynn (5)
25 Scrape (7)

DOWN

1 Talking bird (5)
2 Splash out (7)
3 African hardwood (5)
4 Essence, being (6)
5 Fatty (7)
6 Within (prefix) (5)
7 Vocalists (7)
12 Continuous fire (7)
13 In the middle (7)
15 Plain (7)
16 Talks (6)
18 Sweetener (5)
20 Absolute (5)
21 Door-lock (5)

54

ACROSS

1 Gossip (4)
4 Gobbler (6)
7 —— Gardner (films) (3)
9 Prison (sl.) (4)
10 Off-break (cricket) (8)
11 —— G (comic) (3)
12 Sir —— Guinness (4)
13 Glass cylinder (4-4)
16 Inland sea (13)
19 Incidentally (2,3,3)
23 Bare (4)
24 —— Angeles (3)
25 Pearl can (anag.) (8)
26 Stepped (4)
27 Sticky stuff (sl.) (3)
28 Dry sausage (6)
29 Small horse (4)

DOWN

2 Gunner (12)
3 Pakistan's commercial centre (7)
4 Silent (5)
5 Scoffs (5)
6 Precise (5)
8 Devoted old couple (5,3,4)
14 Not late or betimes (5)
15 —— for Two (song) (3)
17 Golf peg (3)
18 Uninterrupted (3-4)
20 Hi ! (5)
21 Housey-housey (5)
22 Gray's —— (poem) (5)

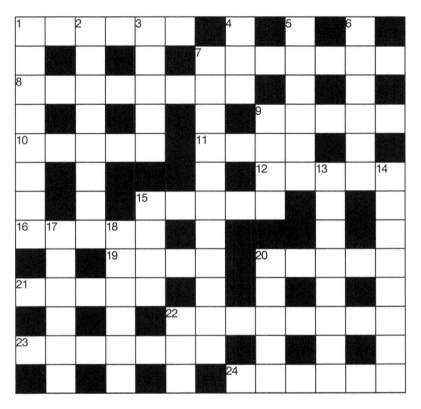

ACROSS

1 Agitation (6)
7 Ruled (7)
8 Clergyman (8)
9 Trap (5)
10 Period of watch (5)
11 Chilled (4)
12 Wretched (5)
15 Chart (5)
16 Church land (5)
19 Figure-skating jump (4)
20 Take a dip (5)
21 Rime (5)
22 Airy (8)
23 Parallelism (7)
24 Search (anag.) (6)

DOWN

1 Still (8)
2 Turncoat (8)
3 Agave fibre (5)
4 Through (3)
5 Schedule (6)
6 Rue (6)
7 Trustworthiness (11)
9 Dried up (4)
13 Gauche (8)
14 Falsetto singer (8)
15 Bible passage (4)
17 Voice-box (6)
18 Volcanic rock (6)
20 Copper —— (tree) (5)
22 Ovum (3)

56

ACROSS

1 Packet-boat (5)
4 Follows (5)
10 Post-mortem (7)
11 Carried (5)
12 Freight (5)
13 Correspondence (7)
15 Above (4)
17 Rub (5)
19 Nous (5)
22 Require (4)
25 Waterfall (7)
27 Association (5)
29 Throw (5)
30 Envisage (7)
31 Revolt (5)
32 Roadside (5)

DOWN

2 Come in (5)
3 Rebuke (7)
5 Church figure (5)
6 Bounty (7)
7 Broad comedy (5)
8 Bike (5)
9 Banquet (5)
14 Gaelic (4)
16 Sell (4)
18 The soil (anag.) (7)
20 Teach (7)
21 Jeer (5)
23 Weird (5)
24 Below (5)
26 Corner; fish (5)
28 Sweet topping (5)

ACROSS

1 Dr Jekyll's alter ego (4)
3 Makes merry (8)
9 Additional clause (5)
10 Touching at a single point (7)
11 Moose (3)
13 Word-finder, dictionary (9)
14 Rover; forest warden (6)
16 Enthusiastically (6)
18 Sweet smell (9)
20 Attention (3)
22 Runaway lovers (7)
23 Backless sofa (5)
25 Wavering (8)
26 Influence (4)

DOWN

1 Vast crowd (5)
2 Counterfeit (3)
4 Beginning (6)
5 Family tree (7)
6 Headroom (9)
7 Fulfil, appease (7)
8 Court order (4)
12 Marsupials (9)
14 Brace, enliven (7)
15 Serious, resolute (7)
17 Agreement (6)
19 Ambitions (4)
21 Gangling (5)
24 Promise (3)

58

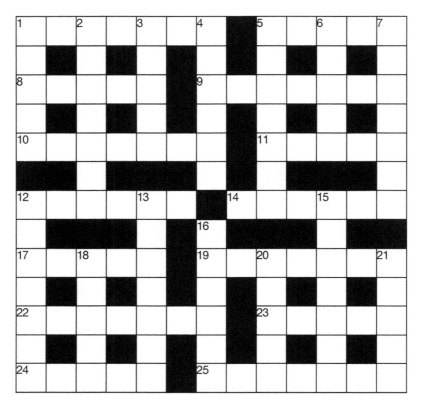

ACROSS

1 Musical performance (7)
5 Pulls forcibly (5)
8 Love goddess; planet (5)
9 Slovenly (7)
10 Mitigate (7)
11 Surpass (5)
12 Scuffle (6)
14 Waterproof jacket (6)
17 Prevent (5)
19 Archaic (7)
22 Unplait (anag.) (7)
23 Wind spirally (5)
24 —— Terry, actress (5)
25 Quandary (7)

DOWN

1 Insurance (5)
2 Confound (7)
3 Follow (5)
4 Bed canopy (6)
5 Whaling spear (7)
6 In poor shape (5)
7 Shakespearean money-lender (7)
12 Apprentice (7)
13 Balt (7)
15 Funeral mass (7)
16 Was unsuccessful (6)
18 Drive out (5)
20 Complete (5)
21 More (5)

ACROSS

1 More stable (6)
4 Intended (5)
8 Manages (5)
9 Biblical city (7)
10 Diminishes (7)
11 Sickly-sweet (4)
12 Salt pork (3)
14 Face cover (4)
15 Encourage (4)
18 Shrill bark (3)
21 Competent (4)
23 Fur-bearing animal (7)
25 Light shoes (7)
26 Japanese martial art (5)
27 Faithful (5)
28 Harmony (6)

DOWN

1 Easy, fluent (6)
2 Repartee (7)
3 Stray eel (anag.) (8)
4 —— *Dick* (4)
5 Permit (5)
6 Painful when touched (6)
7 Disconcert, embarrass (5)
13 Inhabitant of Oz (8)
16 Coffee dregs (7)
17 Medieval retainer (6)
19 Flatten (5)
20 Innate (6)
22 Tall and lean (5)
24 Dance (4)

60

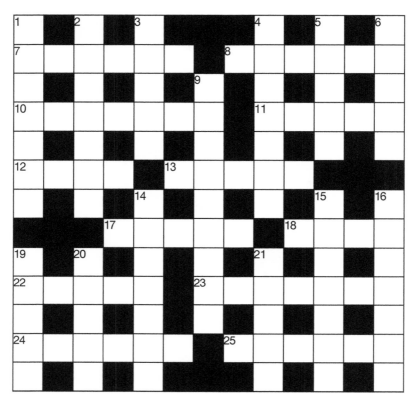

ACROSS

7 Series of games (6)
8 Bohemians (6)
10 *La Dolce Vita* director; I fell in (anag.) (7)
11 Housey-Housey (5)
12 Underdone (4)
13 Exclude (5)
17 Toy bear (5)
18 Donated (4)
22 Blustery (5)
23 *Stormy* —— (song) (7)
24 Gambols (6)
25 Senior nurse (6)

DOWN

1 Likes better (7)
2 —— & Héloise (7)
3 Start (5)
4 Flowering shrubs (7)
5 Perceptive (5)
6 Royal race meeting (5)
9 Bed cover (9)
14 US city and state (3,4)
15 Begets (7)
16 Deriding (7)
19 Times two (5)
20 Marsh bird (5)
21 The Land of the Rising Sun (5)

ACROSS

1 Writing instrument (6)
4 Chekhov's *Uncle* —— (5)
8 Game-bird (5)
9 1960s hairstyle (7)
10 Riddles (7)
11 Bill of fare (4)
12 Flow back (3)
14 Type of melon (4)
15 Continent (4)
18 Consume (3)
21 Reflected sound (4)
23 Petition (7)
25 Slanting (7)
26 Avoid (5)
27 Hawaiian goodbye (5)
28 Up-slope (6)

DOWN

1 32-card game (6)
2 Inn rage (anag.) (7)
3 Elucidate (8)
4 Vista (4)
5 Ingenuous (5)
6 eg 5th (New York) (6)
7 Maltreat (5)
13 Feasts (8)
16 Coolant for drink (3,4)
17 Basque ball game (6)
19 Endeavoured (5)
20 eg 42nd (New York) (6)
22 Hi ! (5)
24 —— *fortis* (4)

62

ACROSS

1 22 yards (5)
4 God (Hebrew) (7)
8 Passage (7)
9 Scottish lakes (5)
10 —— Agassi (5)
11 Inspiring dread (7)
13 Sweet, green plum (4)
15 Soft mud (6)
17 Wall painting (6)
20 Curse (4)
22 Soviet farming unit (7)
24 Unexpurgated (5)
26 Musical instrument (5)
27 Mother of pearl (7)
28 New baby's clothes (8)
29 Commonplace (5)

DOWN

1 Short broadsword (7)
2 Prize (5)
3 Savings (4,3)
4 Effect of long flight (3,3)
5 Divide by two (5)
6 Empty-headed (7)
7 Speed (5)
12 Warp and —— (4)
14 A long time (4)
16 Not masculine (7)
18 Long stringy fruit (7)
19 Ground cereal (7)
21 Put air into (6)
22 Small secret group (5)
23 German submarine (1-4)
25 Jester (5)

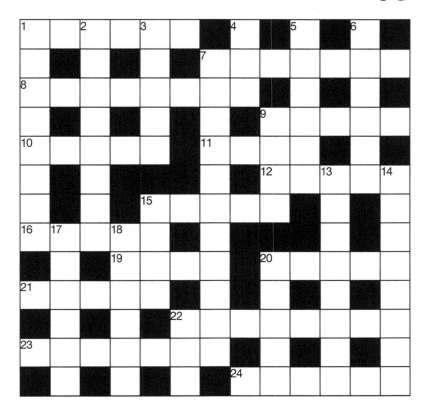

ACROSS

1 Meagre (6)
7 Agriculturalists (7)
8 Furniture maker (8)
9 Spiteful (5)
10 Godliness (5)
11 Churl (4)
12 Stem; track down (5)
15 Likely to tremble (5)
16 Under strain (5)
19 Tableland (4)
20 Do without (5)
21 Innate aptitude (5)
22 Acclaim (8)
23 Wax lyrical (7)
24 Spirit (6)

DOWN

1 Travel permit (8)
2 Vassal (8)
3 Prepared (5)
4 Woodland god (3)
5 Armpit (anag.) (6)
6 Senselessly cruel (6)
7 Tolerance (11)
9 Snug (4)
13 Diverging from normality (8)
14 Paraffin oil (9)
15 Prophet (4)
17 West London borough (6)
18 Forge (6)
20 Became icy (5)
22 Venomous snake (3)

64

ACROSS

1 South coast resort (8)
7 In good time (5)
8 Guardsman (9)
9 *Princess* —— (Gilbert & Sullivan) (3)
10 Short letter (4)
11 Shellfish (6)
13 Verses (6)
14 Permeable by fluids (6)
17 Mythological Greek she-monster (6)
18 Network (4)
20 Peckham —— (3)
22 Barren (9)
23 Test (5)
24 Blood-feud (8)

DOWN

1 Commence (5)
2 Clumsily (7)
3 Cure (4)
4 Repugnant (6)
5 Delicate, feeble (5)
6 Spins round (7)
7 Oi, senor! (anag.) (7)
12 Badly frighten (7)
13 Go back (7)
15 Gorge oneself (7)
16 A standard unit (6)
17 Decorative plaster (5)
19 *Old Testament* prophet (5)
21 Horse-breeding establishment (4)

ACROSS

1 Encounter (4)
4 Pooh's mournful pal (6)
7 —— Gershwin (3)
9 Tongue of land (4)
10 The Mad Monk (8)
11 Everyone (3)
12 Smile broadly (4)
13 Compliant (8)
16 Diplomatist's rank (13)
19 Irene? TNT ! (anag.) (8)
23 Wise man (4)
24 Limp (3)
25 1815 battle (8)
26 Egg-shaped (4)
27 Hasten (3)
28 Great gun (6)
29 Exploit (4)

DOWN

2 Tentative (12)
3 Fairy queen (7)
4 In good time (5)
5 —— *have no Bananas*! (3,2)
6 Circular (5)
8 Deaf communication (4,8)
14 Likeness (5)
15 Zodiac sign (3)
17 Knight (3)
18 Reply (7)
20 Girl's name (5)
21 Man-made fibre (5)
22 Prickly plant (5)

66

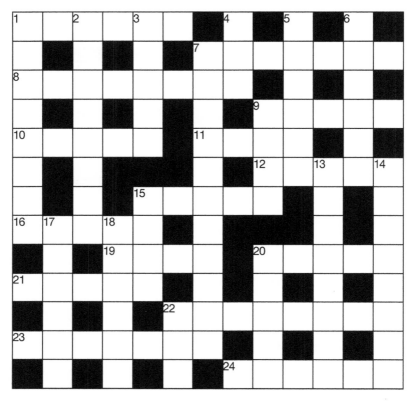

ACROSS

1 Rowing (6)
7 Winding (7)
8 Unearth (8)
9 Gulf state (5)
10 Inn (5)
11 Heavy wooden hammer (4)
12 Wakes (anag.) (5)
15 Sticky (5)
16 Light beer (5)
19 Very bright star (4)
20 Thread (5)
21 Ceiling beam (5)
22 Accommodation at 9 *down* (8)
23 Tynesider (7)
24 Greek isle (6)

DOWN

1 Examine and repair (8)
2 Repeating aloud (8)
3 Umbilicus (5)
4 Mimic (3)
5 Tests (6)
6 Body of new recruits (6)
7 Abdominal pain (11)
9 Landing-place (4)
13 Part of a piano (8)
14 Radio (8)
15 Jog (4)
17 Portuguese islands (6)
18 Guarantee (6)
20 Scottish river (5)
22 Hairpiece (3)

ACROSS

1 Noise (5)
4 Wide bay, eg German (5)
10 Enrage (7)
11 VIII (5)
12 White heron (5)
13 Captures (7)
15 Lady's fingers (4)
17 Small giraffe-like animal (5)
19 Strive (5)
22 Insane (4)
25 Overshadow (7)
27 Wrath (5)
29 Spicy cookery style (5)
30 Inauspicious (7)
31 Sinatra song (2,3)
32 Liquorice seed (5)

DOWN

2 Happen (5)
3 Uninterrupted (3-4)
5 Sluggish (5)
6 Insincere nonsense (7)
7 £5 (5)
8 Peggy Lee song (5)
9 Hiding-place (5)
14 Socially crass (sl.) (4)
16 Teases (colloq.) (4)
18 Party-pooper (7)
20 I, a Latin? (anag.) (7)
21 40-40 (5)
23 Fable writer (5)
24 Money (sl.) (5)
26 Police car (5)
28 144 (5)

68

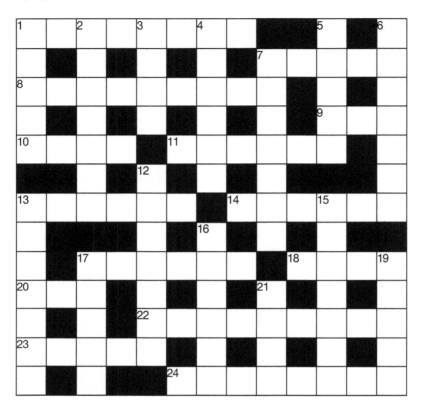

ACROSS

1 Greek god of sleep (8)
7 Mischievous legendary beings (5)
8 County (9)
9 Unwell (3)
10 Ship's company (4)
11 Make the rounds (6)
13 Upshot (6)
14 Right to approach (6)
17 Social position (6)
18 Shape (4)
20 Deed (3)
22 pm (9)
23 Pick-me-up (5)
24 Gem (8)

DOWN

1 Imitate (5)
2 Compensate (7)
3 Ship's cargo space (4)
4 Oust from parliament (6)
5 Be of use (5)
6 Futile (7)
7 Pluck out, remove (7)
12 Yearly calendar (7)
13 Boat race meeting (7)
15 Thrift (7)
16 Tradition (6)
17 Foul smell (5)
19 French impressionist painter (5)
21 Worry (4)

ACROSS

1 More distant (7)
8 Bodily shape (6)
9 Norfolk's capital (7)
11 Impeded (8)
12 Trap (5)
14 Whirlpool (4)
15 Story-teller (8)
17 Religious study (8)
18 Anthony Eden, Earl of
—— (4)
20 Watchful (5)
21 French composer (8)
23 Extinct (7)
24 Bill; observe (6)
25 Ripped off (7)

DOWN

2 Be plentiful (6)
3 Tastelessly gaudy (6)
4 Every (4)
5 Frolic (7)
6 Profitable (9)
7 Anti-perspirant (9)
10 Addressed forcibly (9)
12 Mawkish emotion (9)
13 Hardship (9)
16 Verbal ease (7)
18 Attraction (6)
19 Carole (anag.) (6)
22 Small duck (4)

70

ACROSS

1 Devoured (5)
4 Anger, bile (6)
9 Beau —— (7)
10 Flower (5)
11 Garden tool (4)
12 Normal (7)
13 Two-wheel carriage (3)
14 You (4)
16 Runnel (4)
18 Deciduous tree (3)
20 Shellfish (7)
21 Heroic tale (4)
24 Left-hand page (5)
25 Given, having (7)
26 Neglectful (6)
27 Unpleasant (5)

DOWN

1 Board ship (6)
2 Lorry (5)
3 Cognomen (4)
5 School holiday (4-4)
6 Sideways (7)
7 Steal cattle (6)
8 Colloquial jargon (5)
13 Magnanimous (8)
15 Dull, commonplace (7)
17 Lapwing (6)
18 Surrey town (5)
19 Sourly (6)
22 Welsh county (5)
23 Norse god (4)

ACROSS

1 Sawbones (7)
5 Rum —— (cake) (4)
7 What Laurel called Hardy (5)
8 Chessman (6)
10 Sharp (4)
11 Judgment (8)
13 Published (6)
14 Pat toe (anag.) (6)
17 Stress (8)
19 The Spanish —— (4)
21 Homicide (6)
22 —— frutti (5)
23 Network (4)
24 Song-like (7)

DOWN

1 Accumulated supplies (10)
2 Long waves (7)
3 Always (4)
4 Japanese stock index (6)
5 Stiff hairs (8)
6 Brendan —— (Irish author) (5)
9 100th anniversary (10)
12 Had raven (anag.) (8)
15 Mouldable (7)
16 Dee/Mersey peninsula (6)
18 Short break (5)
20 Heavenly body (4)

72

ACROSS

1 Sidney —— , Fabian (4)
4 Spectacles (6)
7 Din (3)
9 Portico (4)
10 Marginal (anag.) (8)
11 Conflict (3)
12 Indigo dye (4)
13 More gloomy (8)
16 Fourfold (13)
19 Gather (8)
23 Fury (4)
24 Shelter (3)
25 Apart (8)
26 Destiny (4)
27 Antelope (3)
28 Sweater (6)
29 Skulk (4)

DOWN

2 Quenched (12)
3 Fought rowdily (7)
4 Green turf (5)
5 Eat grass (5)
6 West Country river (5)
8 Detective (12)
14 Repulse (5)
15 —— Baba (3)
17 Tup (3)
18 Cautious (7)
20 Dodge (5)
21 Orchestral section (5)
22 Pensive poem (5)

ACROSS

1 Woo (5)
4 Touch down (6)
9 Young child (7)
10 Ravine (5)
11 Frolic; bird (4)
12 Flagrant (7)
13 Appeal for assistance (3)
14 Gravel (4)
16 Profound (4)
18 Talk; fuel (3)
20 Determination (7)
21 Past (4)
24 Representative (5)
25 Book; store (7)
26 People (6)
27 Reside (5)

DOWN

1 Cows (6)
2 Beneath (5)
3 Lofty (4)
5 Glad-rags (anag.) (8)
6 Rubbish (7)
7 Score (6)
8 Snatches (5)
13 Slender dagger (8)
15 Honour (7)
17 Decree (6)
18 Literary or artistic style (5)
19 Trial (6)
22 Poetry (5)
23 Secondhand (4)

74

ACROSS

1 Protect (5)
4 Degree of thickness (7)
8 Naval officer (7)
9 Wizened, wrinkled (5)
10 Language of India (5)
11 Widespread (7)
13 Want (4)
15 Rock-bound, jagged (6)
17 Female companion for men in Japan (6)
20 Ended (4)
22 Prevailing trend (7)
24 Cuban dance (5)
26 Battleground (5)
27 Meadow pipit (7)
28 Power, capacity (7)
29 In-car (anag.) (5)

DOWN

1 Vividly described (7)
2 Capital of Jordan (5)
3 A favourite (7)
4 Great flood (6)
5 Synthetic yarn (5)
6 Internal organs (7)
7 Swiss mountain call (5)
12 Rim (4)
14 Small island (4)
16 Food (7)
18 Irregular (7)
19 Of the US 49th state (7)
21 Church room for garments (6)
22 Embrace (5)
23 Once more (5)
25 Florida tourist resort (5)

ACROSS

1 Advance (4)
4 Progenitors (7)
8 Trade (8)
9 Vigour (3)
11 Shropshire town (6)
13 Fuel (6)
14 Outmoded (5)
15 Cylindrical container (4)
17 Arboreal knot (4)
18 Buxom lass (5)
20 Wild ass (6)
21 Recluse (6)
24 Eggs (3)
25 Operatic text (8)
26 School bag (7)
27 Nagging pain (4)

DOWN

2 Egg-shaped (5)
3 OT hunter (6)
4 Extra benefit (4)
5 Stank (6)
6 French lamb casserole (7)
7 Likeness (10)
10 Very greedy (10)
12 Hesitate (5)
13 Fish; roosting-place (5)
16 Flagrant (7)
18 Opulence (6)
19 Adhere (anag.) (6)
22 Contest (5)
23 Old Greek coin (4)

76

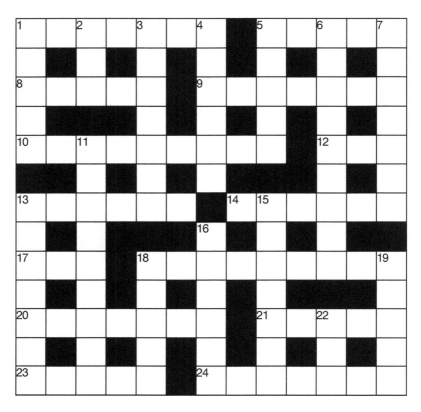

ACROSS

1 Make wider (7)
5 Flight (5)
8 Type of duck (5)
9 Without weapons (7)
10 South London district (9)
12 Nothing (3)
13 Salutes (6)
14 Israeli secret service (6)
17 —— de Janeiro (3)
18 Reclining (9)
20 Easy to read (7)
21 Regretful (5)
23 —— *Grey* (Anne Bronte) (5)
24 Least difficult (7)

DOWN

1 Consecrate (5)
2 Ancient (3)
3 Sleeping (7)
4 Nothing (6)
5 Consternation (5)
6 Recount past events (9)
7 Walked in ungainly fashion (7)
11 Harmonium (4-5)
13 Great ape (7)
15 Gradual assimilation (7)
16 Assent (6)
18 Garments (5)
19 Lovers' meeting (5)
22 Fish eggs (3)

ACROSS

1 Norfolk town (4)
4 Rider (6)
7 Aliens' craft (3)
9 German river (4)
10 Nicer (8)
11 —— up! (3)
12 Lies (anag) (4)
13 Terriers (8)
16 Men's evening wear (6,7)
19 Mishap (8)
23 Indifferent (2-2)
24 Astern (3)
25 Footmen (8)
26 Bawl (4)
27 Digit (3)
28 Twist (6)
29 Youths (4)

DOWN

2 Not clearly (12)
3 Ship's doctor (7)
4 Jests (5)
5 African republic (5)
6 Israeli resort (5)
8 —— *Discs* (BBC) (6,6)
14 Louisiana cookery style (5)
15 Twitch (3)
17 Close (3)
18 Hawk (7)
20 Interior (5)
21 Leave of absence (5)
22 Small portion (5)

78

ACROSS

1 Distinctive (7)
5 Dyke builder (4)
7 Animal life (5)
8 Men from Greece (6)
10 Greek letter (4)
11 Nomad (8)
13 Requisition (6)
14 Hidden (6)
17 Childhood home of Jesus (8)
19 Deep place; abyss (4)
21 Do a favour (6)
22 Fore(finger) (5)
23 Numerous (4)
24 Family (7)

DOWN

1 Enough (10)
2 Regarded as equal (7)
3 —— the Terrible (4)
4 Impasse (3-3)
5 Exaggerated (8)
6 Indian wonder-worker (5)
9 Impaled (10)
12 Iniquity; vastness (8)
15 South American country (7)
16 Skater (anag.) (6)
18 African animal (5)
20 Leo (4)

ACROSS

1 Brisk pace (6)
4 Small fruit (5)
8 Join (5)
9 Naval officer (7)
10 Flaw (7)
11 Despondent (4)
12 Hearing organ (3)
14 Net (4)
15 Reverberate (4)
18 Knot (3)
21 Criticise, fish (4)
23 A strain (anag.) (7)
25 Young hare (7)
26 Lift (5)
27 Wander (5)
28 Most strange (6)

DOWN

1 Plump (6)
2 Ingenuousness (7)
3 Vision (8)
4 Strike against (4)
5 Bucolic (5)
6 Shouted (6)
7 Turning machine (5)
13 Reinstated (8)
16 Inimical (7)
17 Balance; mounts (6)
19 Soil (5)
20 Agitation (6)
22 Waterway (5)
24 Military force (4)

80

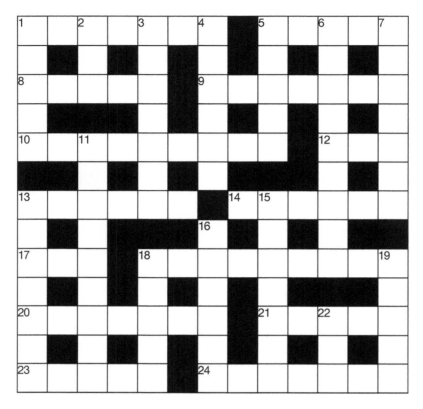

ACROSS

1 Cooperate, contribute (5,2)
5 Pulled by rope (5)
8 Pulsate (5)
9 Artist (7)
10 Brutal, cruel (9)
12 Female fowl (3)
13 Demesne (6)
14 Disregard (6)
17 Fruit of rose plant (3)
18 Erudition (9)
20 Moreover (7)
21 Stroll (5)
23 Implements (5)
24 Raffle, gamble (7)

DOWN

1 Protective covering for an eye (5)
2 Seaman (3)
3 Abode, natural home (7)
4 Male relative (6)
5 Reverse side of coin (5)
6 Rallying cry, slogan (9)
7 Throw into disorder (7)
11 Course in Italian meal (9)
13 Display (7)
15 Manful and brave (7)
16 Crumb, scrap (6)
18 Acclaim, glory (5)
19 Foe (5)
22 Insect (3)

ACROSS

1 Critic (7)
5 Spell (4)
7 Savour (5)
8 Doze (6)
10 Frolic (4)
11 Manifold (8)
13 Disc jockey (6)
14 Spinet (anag.) (6)
17 Extricate (8)
19 Bovine animals (4)
21 Ring (6)
22 Seraglio (5)
23 Reality (4)
24 Ray (7)

DOWN

1 Percussion instrument (10)
2 See (7)
3 Understood (4)
4 Bordering on indecency (6)
5 Promoting (8)
6 Unfasten (5)
9 Staying silent (7,3)
12 Panelled woodwork (8)
15 Without duty (3-4)
16 Pincers (6)
18 Marshy pine forest (5)
20 Avoid (4)

82

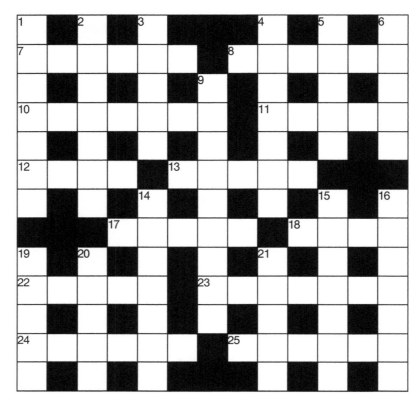

ACROSS

7 Exercises (6)
8 Fiddle about (6)
10 Greed (7)
11 Funereal music (5)
12 Strong wind (4)
13 Command (5)
17 Big (5)
18 Expensive (4)
22 Approximately (5)
23 Trade, vehicles (7)
24 Gipsy (6)
25 Disturbance (6)

DOWN

1 Odd (7)
2 Pale cab (anag.) (7)
3 Ailing (5)
4 Army man (7)
5 Shop (5)
6 Essayed (5)
9 Set apart (9)
14 Durable (7)
15 Exemplary (7)
16 Exact (7)
19 Linger (5)
20 Punctuation mark (5)
21 Wed (5)

ACROSS

1 Put on the scales (5)
4 Marsh marigold (7)
8 Walk unsteadily (7)
9 Shots fired in unison (5)
10 Permit (5)
11 Endocrine gland (7)
13 Locality (4)
15 By more (anag.) (6)
17 Undo (6)
20 Cushiony (4)
22 Pistol case (7)
24 Custom (5)
26 Sudden forward motion (5)
27 Coal miner (7)
28 Playhouse (7)
29 Rubbish (5)

DOWN

1 Loss by use or natural decay (7)
2 LA nil (anag.) (2,3)
3 Public road (7)
4 Martial art (6)
5 Unpleasant (5)
6 Insensitive (7)
7 Haughty (5)
12 Moiety (4)
14 Flower (4)
16 Equilibrium (7)
18 The Moor of Venice (7)
19 Inborn (7)
21 Divine utterance (6)
22 English composer (5)
23 Delightful surprise (5)
25 Concise (5)

84

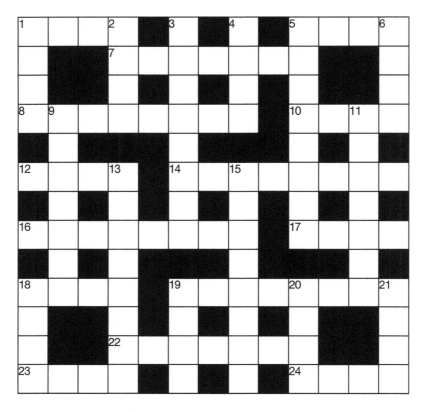

ACROSS

1 Level (4)
5 Drew (4)
7 Formby's instrument (7)
8 Force (8)
10 —— jug (4)
12 Furnishes; seizures (4)
14 Embassy (8)
16 Disciple (8)
17 Tear (anag.) (4)
18 Clenched hand (4)
19 Bibliophile (8)
22 German measles (7)
23 Salver (7)
24 Ten cents (4)

DOWN

1 Love god (4)
2 Bare (4)
3 One-storey house (8)
4 Third son of Adam (4)
5 Will-maker (8)
6 Refuse to give (4)
9 Libyan capital (7)
11 Cured herring (7)
13 Beneficial (8)
15 Grotesque carving (8)
18 Formal command (4)
19 Infant (4)
20 Old blue dye (4)
21 Bog (4)

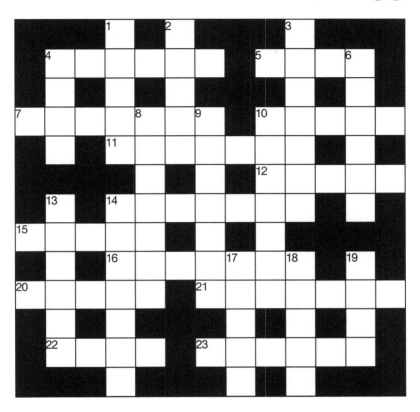

ACROSS

4 Chooser (6)
5 Long-stemmed flower (4)
7 Malicious gossip (7)
10 Saturate, imbue (5)
11 Despotism (7)
12 Wear away (5)
14 Irish ghost (7)
15 Magician (5)
16 Guided (7)
20 Scruffy (5)
21 Girl's name (7)
22 Dreadful (4)
23 Says (6)

DOWN

1 Scarcely sufficient (5)
2 Exclude (5)
3 Mull of —— (7)
4 Rate of speed (4)
6 Cedes (6)
8 Ruling family (7)
9 Catches with noose (7)
10 Coughs and —— spread diseases (7)
13 Risk (6)
14 Large game-bird (7)
17 Corroded (5)
18 Pub game (5)
19 Burden, responsibility (4)

86

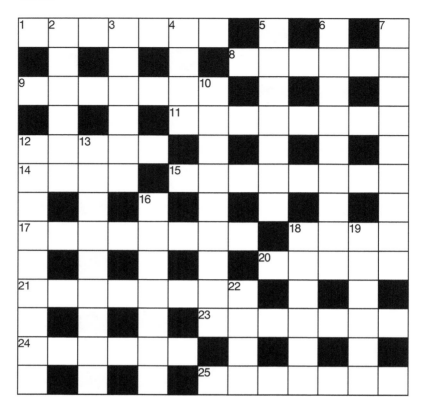

ACROSS

1 Decrepit old cars (7)
8 Catch in a net (6)
9 Throne-stealer (7)
11 —— Holmes (sleuth) (8)
12 Yielded (5)
14 Soon (4)
15 Wrote music (8)
17 Conan Doyle villain (8)
18 Tardy (4)
20 From stem to —— (5)
21 Relate it (anag.) (8)
23 Ladled (7)
24 Gave a gratuity (6)
25 Language of Bangladesh (7)

DOWN

2 *Persuasion* writer (6)
3 Covent —— (6)
4 Regrets (4)
5 Snares (7)
6 Flatfish (5-4)
7 Temporary bed (9)
10 Store hats (anag.) (9)
12 White friar (9)
13 Thick slices of bread (colloq.) (9)
16 Wards off (7)
18 Robust (6)
19 *1984* author (6)
22 Sword (4)

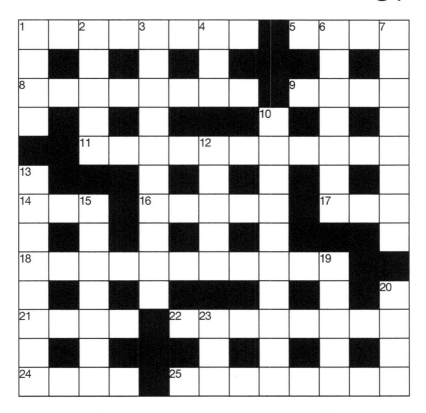

ACROSS

1 Complete (8)
5 So-so (4)
8 Instigating (8)
9 Showy display (4)
11 eg Borstal (11)
14 Clerical vestment (3)
16 Cord (5)
17 Transgression (3)
18 Discreetly (11)
21 Rake (4)
22 Educated (8)
24 eg Fur coat (4)
25 Four-lined verse (8)

DOWN

1 Labour (4)
2 Academy Award (5)
3 Sold out (3,2,5)
4 Alcoholic spirit (3)
6 In love (7)
7 Answering (8)
10 Torrential downpour (10)
12 Large animal (5)
13 Aromatic plant (8)
15 Nomadic Arab (7)
19 Ukrainian port (5)
20 Norse deity (4)
23 Wine vintage (3)

88

ACROSS

1 Less harsh (7)
5 Cloudless (5)
8 Representative (5)
9 Exact (7)
10 Learner (7)
11 In front (5)
12 Useless (6)
14 Insist upon (6)
17 Sugar topping (5)
19 Jobs etc (anag.) (7)
22 Draw (7)
23 Foreign (5)
24 Weird (5)
25 Gist (7)

DOWN

1 Commence (5)
2 Chic (7)
3 Giant (5)
4 Slender sword (6)
5 Leak (7)
6 Ingenuous (5)
7 Ceded (7)
12 Ship (7)
13 Travel-bags (7)
15 Sale (7)
16 Nerve (6)
18 Bury (5)
20 Casual trousers (5)
21 Burn (5)

ACROSS

1 "Hail" in Latin (5)
4 Great tidal wave (7)
8 Dog (7)
9 Finnish bath (5)
10 Barrier (5)
11 Assessor of insurance risks (7)
13 Musical symbol (4)
15 Extent, reach (6)
17 Decorous, modest (6)
20 Piece of information (4)
22 Fighting man (7)
24 North-east Scots town (5)
26 Awaken (5)
27 Heedless, ignorant (7)
28 Sneakiness (7)
29 Simple song (5)

DOWN

1 Schoolbag (7)
2 Ghastly, melodramatic (5)
3 Easy to see (7)
4 Warning (6)
5 Overturn (5)
6 Praise obsequiously (7)
7 European republic (5)
12 Surrender (4)
14 US state (4)
16 Feed and support (7)
18 Gemstone (7)
19 In taut fashion (7)
21 Manger, gutter (6)
22 Factory (5)
23 Utopian (5)
25 Ogre (5)

90

ACROSS

1 Scorch (4)
4 Gullible person (6)
7 Play a role (3)
9 North Pacific island (4)
10 Lawless (8)
11 Atmosphere; dry (3)
12 Roman poet (4)
13 Plea (8)
16 Malicious gossip (13)
19 Reputation (8)
23 Trial (4)
24 Second person (3)
25 Blarney (4-4)
26 Scottish dance (4)
27 Ocean (3)
28 Stylish (6)
29 Wound dressing (4)

DOWN

2 Ambiguity (12)
3 Muslim month of fasting (7)
4 Aster (anag.) (5)
5 Cunning (5)
6 Host (5)
8 Ludwig ——, philosopher (12)
14 Artificial fibre (5)
15 Greek "r" (3)
17 Failure (3)
18 Unaffected (7)
20 Of birth (5)
21 Devotional paintings (5)
22 Romany (5)

ACROSS

1 eg Pines (5)
4 Inciting (6)
9 Repartee (7)
10 Fire-raising (5)
11 Friend, partner (4)
12 Sportsman (7)
13 Mate (3)
14 Cicatrice (4)
16 Obtains (4)
18 WWII women's army corps (3)
20 Accumulated (7)
21 Prison (sl) (4)
24 Indian language group (5)
25 Sideways (7)
26 & 27 Thurber's daydreamer (6,5)

DOWN

1 Plaid (6)
2 Throw out (5)
3 Neither good nor bad (2-2)
5 Selfish drivers (8)
6 Look over (7)
7 Seabird (6)
8 eg Iron (5)
13 Immaculate (8)
15 Strait (7)
17 Kind of nut (6)
18 Grown-up (5)
19 Ruffled (6)
22 Fortune-telling cards (5)
23 Article (4)

92

ACROSS

1 Pet rodent (7)
5 Curse (4)
7 & 8 Eraser (5,6)
10 Nat King —— (mus.) (4)
11 Flower sellers (8)
13 Tried out (6)
14 Sensitive (6)
17 A pure one (anag.) (8)
19 Scrutinise (4)
21 Very drunk or drugged (sl.) (6)
22 Market-place (5)
23 Peepers (sl.) (4)
24 The science of language (7)

DOWN

1 Barber (10)
2 Interferes (7)
3 Hard wood (4)
4 Seldom (6)
5 Red beard (anag.) (8)
6 Encounters (5)
9 Stargazer (10)
12 Portions (8)
15 Decency (7)
16 eg a Chihuahua (6)
18 Moley's friend (5)
20 —— 's Dyke (4)

ACROSS

1 Large rock (7)
8 Extra in cricket (2-4)
9 Killed by a mob (7)
11 Unfolded (8)
12 Allude (5)
14 Outstanding person (4)
15 Dispersion of a people (8)
17 Class of protein (8)
18 Interdict (4)
20 Hoarder (5)
21 Cooling (8)
23 Melting (7)
24 Pompous (6)
25 Thaw, melt (7)

DOWN

2 Gas (6)
3 Box (6)
4 Saw (4)
5 Unemployed (7)
6 Idle person (9)
7 Roman fighter (9)
10 Lacking (9)
12 Pebbledash (9)
13 Savage (9)
16 Make suitable (7)
18 Observer (6)
19 Sent in (anag.) (6)
22 Clarified buffalo butter (4)

94

ACROSS

1 Ethical (5)
4 Straighten (5)
10 Book (7)
11 Dig (5)
12 Overweight (5)
13 Meet (7)
15 River of Hades (4)
17 Inscribe (5)
19 Soil (5)
22 Female relation (4)
25 Occidental (7)
27 Characteristic (5)
29 Finished (5)
30 The race (anag.) (7)
31 Tired (5)
32 Narrative (5)

DOWN

2 Children (5)
3 Most difficult (7)
5 Burdened (5)
6 Valiant (7)
7 Endure (5)
8 Clemency (5)
9 Moorland (5)
14 Cattle (4)
16 Rip (4)
18 Remains (7)
20 Win, draw (7)
21 Possessor (5)
23 Oneness (5)
24 Begin (5)
26 Senior (5)
28 Detest (5)

ACROSS

1 Makes boat watertight (6)
4 Sea-trip for pleasure (6)
7 Abode of a recluse (9)
9 Search for (4)
10 Needle-case (4)
11 Majestic (5)
13 Evening meal (6)
14 Commemorative plate (6)
15 Angelic child (6)
17 Glowing coals (6)
19 Cuttlefish pigment (5)
20 Insect (4)
22 Pace (4)
23 Connoisseur of wines (9)
24 In short supply (6)
25 Boil gently (6)

DOWN

1 Population count (6)
2 Emblem of Wales (4)
3 Silly smile (6)
4 Short sleep (6)
5 Incite (4)
6 Arouse (6)
7 Magic words (3-6)
8 Correct behaviour (9)
11 Romulus's twin (5)
12 Beast of burden (5)
15 College area (6)
16 Formerly (6)
17 Boat crews (6)
18 Private in the Royal Engineers (6)
21 Listen to (4)
22 Slender (4)

96

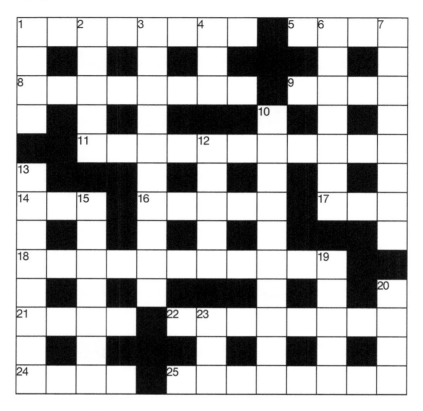

ACROSS

1 Holland gin (8)
5 Photo (4)
8 Welcoming (8)
9 Stuff (4)
11 X-ray expert (11)
14 Intimidate; bovine female (3)
16 New —— , the Indian capital (5)
17 Longing (3)
18 Lover of France (11)
21 Bacchanal (4)
22 US lawyer (8)
24 Consider (4)
25 Isn't ripe (anag.) (8)

DOWN

1 Satirical revue (4)
2 Dither (5)
3 Self-taught person (10)
4 Play on words (3)
6 Appal (7)
7 Enticing (8)
10 Concerned (10)
12 Type of primula (5)
13 Execution platform (8)
15 Noisy dispute (7)
19 Boredom (5)
20 Cowshed (4)
23 Bituminous substance (3)

ACROSS

1 Crooked, amiss (4)
5 Upper-class man (sl.) (4)
7 Subjugate (7)
8 Sailing ships (8)
10 Handle roughly (4)
12 Roman poet (4)
14 Inexhaustible, unlimited (8)
16 Show nose (anag.) (8)
17 Painful, tender (4)
18 Chain of rocks (4)
19 Reserve (3,5)
22 Erudite (7)
23 Aquatic mammal (4)
24 Old Ireland (4)

DOWN

1 Excited, expectant (4)
2 Bawl (4)
3 Greatly surprise (8)
4 4th planet from the Sun (4)
5 Ending point (8)
6 Sense (4)
9 Go forward (7)
11 Spoke (7)
13 Ruin (8)
15 Worrying (8)
18 Arguments; tiers (4)
19 Pole (4)
20 Team (4)
21 Gain (4)

98

ACROSS

1 Genii (5)
4 Card game (5)
10 Bowling game (7)
11 Card game (5)
12 Zest (5)
13 Dozing (7)
15 Wise men (4)
17 VII (5)
19 Big (5)
22 Playthings (4)
25 Warrior (7)
27 The Queen of —— from the *Old Testament* (5)
29 Violent attack (5)
30 So soon? (7)
31 Money-lending (5)
32 Cricket trophy (5)

DOWN

1 *Dad's Army* corporal (5)
3 Offensive (7)
5 Still single (5)
6 Posting (7)
7 Male deer (5)
8 Employing (5)
9 Platform (5)
14 Greasy (4)
16 Poker stake (4)
18 Listens (anag.) (7)
20 Declares (7)
21 —— Villa (sport) (5)
23 eg Ear (5)
24 Woodland god (5)
26 Bury (5)
28 Rub out (5)

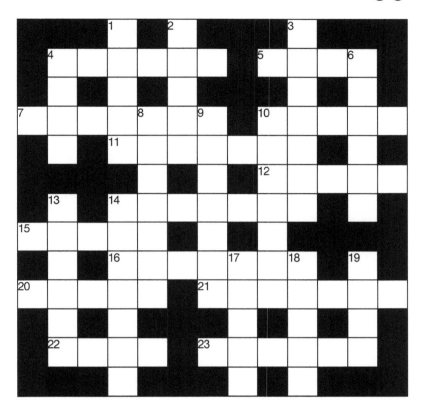

ACROSS

4 Larger (6)
5 Thin fog (4)
7 Essential oil (7)
10 Large fruit (5)
11 Stood on high (7)
12 Enemy (5)
14 Reveal (7)
15 Gemstone (5)
16 Pickling (7)
20 Hot dry wind (5)
21 Language of the Philippines (7)
22 Row (4)
23 Protest (6)

DOWN

1 Luxor's country (5)
2 Beneath (5)
3 Indefinitely adjourned (4,3)
4 Heehaw (4)
6 Insect's upper body (6)
8 Skyline (7)
9 Demand (7)
10 Amalgamating (7)
13 Tint (6)
14 Shading (anag.) (7)
17 Metrical feet (5)
18 Small hammer (5)
19 Jerk (4)

100

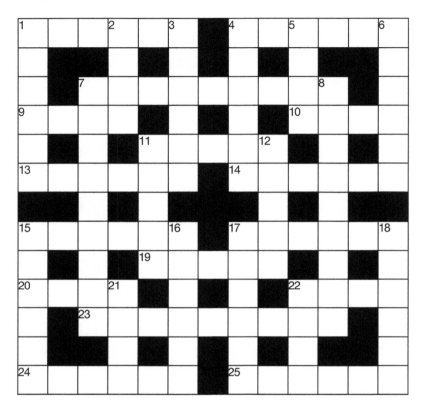

ACROSS

1 Wrote (6)
4 Mythical monster (6)
7 Saccharine (9)
9 Love god (4)
10 Solitary (4)
11 Warning traffic-light (5)
13 Crave water (6)
14 Small boat (6)
15 Cooked in water (6)
17 Encase (anag.) (6)
19 Females (5)
20 Insurrection (4)
22 Froth (4)
23 Icelandic capital (9)
24 Peddler (6)
25 Vigour (6)

DOWN

1 Obvious (6)
2 Current affairs (4)
3 Imagined (6)
4 Considered (6)
5 Cain's victim (4)
6 Subtle distinction (6)
7 Lawyer (9)
8 Oil-rig worker (9)
11 Awry (5)
12 Mature (5)
15 Beetroot soup (6)
16 Stevedore (6)
17 Upper house (6)
18 Hostility (6)
21 Hardwood (4)
22 Pretentiousness (4)

ACROSS

1 Cat's vibrating sound (4)
5 Glove (4)
7 Unappreciative person (7)
8 Patellae (8)
10 Orderly (4)
12 Clasp, part of padlock (4)
14 Grow in size (8)
16 Grecian (8)
17 Expectorate (4)
18 Leading actor (4)
19 Palliasse (8)
22 Beginnings (7)
23 Midday (4)
24 Mountain lake (4)

DOWN

1 eg Rose (4)
2 Annoy, irritate (4)
3 Relating to the land (8)
4 Go by (4)
5 Wanders (8)
6 Lean (4)
9 Proximate (7)
11 Attacks (7)
13 Despicable coward (8)
15 Mixed drink (8)
18 Indication (4)
19 Post (4)
20 Repose (4)
21 In a short time (4)

102

ACROSS

1 Master of Ceremonies (colloq.) (5)
4 Multiplied by itself (7)
8 Trembles (7)
9 Bestowed (5)
10 Japanese porcelain (5)
11 Tolerated (7)
13 Designation (4)
15 E (6)
17 Puzzle (6)
20 Berkshire college (4)
22 Acupressure (7)
24 Fortune-telling cards (5)
26 Quits (5)
27 All vain (anag.) (7)
28 Missives (7)
29 Arab republic (5)

DOWN

1 Ask (7)
2 Dame —— Butt (mus.) (5)
3 Twilight (7)
4 Method, plan (6)
5 Incited (5)
6 Venerated (7)
7 Ate (5)
12 Roman emperor (4)
14 The —— have it (4)
16 Distinguished (7)
18 Concentrated (7)
19 Tax cert (anag.) (7)
21 Sods (6)
22 Aroma (5)
23 Sense (5)
25 Revive (5)

ACROSS

1 Talent (4)
4 Caught (7)
8 African country (8)
9 Flow (3)
11 Divulge (3,3)
13 Golden fruit (6)
14 Light entertainment (5)
15 Bay (4)
17 Develop (4)
18 Rough (5)
20 Inner tower (6)
21 Mood (6)
24 Cask (3)
25 Acting in a small way (8)
26 Angered (anag.) (7)
27 German wine (4)

DOWN

2 Dolt (5)
3 Small drum (6)
4 Brass instrument (4)
5 Boulevard (6)
6 Colleague (7)
7 Drudgery (6-4)
10 Explained (10)
12 One from the Lone Star state (5)
13 Pursuit (5)
16 Isle of Wight resort (7)
18 Tomboy (6)
19 Fitness (6)
22 Great alarm (5)
23 Woodwind instrument (4)

104

ACROSS

1 Chortle (7)
5 Rowing crew (5)
8 Frock (5)
9 Penchant (7)
10 Coercion (9)
12 View (3)
13 Corpulent (6)
14 Renowned (6)
17 Newt (3)
18 Fatuity (9)
20 Incise (7)
21 Throng (5)
23 Entice (5)
24 Oriental (7)

DOWN

1 Apple drink (5)
2 Employ (3)
3 Bird of prey (7)
4 French pastry (6)
5 Precise (5)
6 Set to ring (anag.) (9)
7 Big cat (7)
11 Artifice (9)
13 Give; now (7)
15 Lands (7)
16 Assert (6)
18 Commence (5)
19 Strict (5)
22 Cereal (3)

ANSWERS

1

Across

1 Straiten
7 Arrow
8 Audacious
9 Nun
10 Fact
11 Agenda
13 Callow
14 Beagle
17 Coffee
18 Flop
20 Cue
22 Raconteur
23 Drake
24 Announce

Down

1 Staff
2 Radical
3 Inch
4 Enough
5 Arena
6 Dwindle
7 Asunder
12 Bonfire
13 Cascade
15 Galleon
16 Beacon
17 Cedar
19 Purse
21 Anno

2

Across

1 Vietnam
5 Wore
7 Choux
8 Malady
10 Flog
11 Timorous
13 Riyadh
14 Gemini
17 Ugliness
19 Shut
21 Entire
22 Urban
23 Pray
24 Theatre

Down

1 Vociferous
2 Economy
3 Next
4 Memoir
5 Walk-over
6 Radio
9 Assistance
12 Identity
15 Inhibit
16 Aspect
18 Lunar
20 Ruse

3

Across

1 Ease
4 Tenders
8 Abrogate
9 Tor
11 Credit
13 Aegean
14 Crowd
15 Ride
17 Meal
18 Scrub
20 Induce
21 Larkin
24 Ode
25 Tendrils
26 Sangria
27 Last

Down

2 Amble
3 Exotic
4 Teak
5 Needed
6 Extreme
7 Sprinkling
10 Scurrilous
12 Trice
13 Awful
16 Dudgeon
18 Scoter
19 Barrel
22 Kells
23 Inca

4

Across
1 Webb
4 Sights
7 Urn
9 Stun
10 Interval
11 Kip
12 True
13 End-users
16 Cross-dressers
19 Assented
23 Ursa
24 Off
25 Snuggles
26 Fred
27 Ell
28 Prayed
29 Easy

Down
2 Enterprising
3 Bunkers
4 Snipe
5 Gated
6 Terns
8 Hairdressers
14 Nurse
15 Ups
17 Sin
18 Shuffle
20 Eager
21 Telly
22 Dosed

5

Across
1 Soon
5 Army
7 Enlaced
8 Knitwear
10 Quip
12 Swan
14 Nebraska
16 Betrayal
17 Eton
18 Asti
19 Guernsey
22 Showing
23 Gobi
24 Husk

Down
1 Sark
2 Newt
3 Alderney
4 Scar
5 Adequate
6 Yomp
9 Newness
11 Irksome
13 Narcissi
15 Bulletin
18 Agog
19 Goon
20 Nigh
21 Yank

6

Across
1 Bonus
4 Notches
8 Abilene
9 Large
10 Theft
11 Lineage
13 Reed
15 Yonder
17 Effect
20 Star
22 Pitcher
24 Alarm
26 Phial
27 Frigate
28 Legatee
29 Eject

Down
1 Beastly
2 Noise
3 Spectre
4 Needle
5 Talon
6 Herbage
7 Swede
12 Idea
14 Erse
16 Nothing
18 Fragile
19 Tempest
21 Trifle
22 Pupil
23 Holst
25 Agate

7

Across
1 Bait
3 Auvergne
9 Loyal
10 Retinue
11 Ask
13 Desperado
14 Betide
16 Stymie
18 Agitation
20 Spa
22 Dialect
23 Spell
25 Dressing
26 Grow

Down
1 Balsa
2 Ivy
4 Unrest
5 Entreat
6 Gendarmes
7 Eyesore
8 Glad
12 Kittiwake
14 Branded
15 Dealers
17 Listen
19 Nest
21 Allow
24 Ear

8

Across
1 Block
4 Aiding
9 Complex
10 Sense
11 Echo
12 Sirloin
13 Fat
14 Pail
16 Base
18 Sue
20 Trumpet
21 Epée
24 Panda
25 Numeral
26 Ersatz
27 Homer

Down
1 Bicker
2 Oomph
3 Kali
5 Inscribe
6 Igneous
7 Greene
8 Exist
13 Flippant
15 Alumnus
17 Staple
18 Stank
19 Cellar
22 Purim
23 Amah

9

Across
1 Calmer
4 Light
8 Friar
9 Revenge
10 Evening
11 Zero
12 Sag
14 Uses
15 Ruse
18 Toe
21 **& 23** Rory Bremner
25 Andiron
26 Ovary
27 Yarns
28 Denser

Down
1 Coffee
2 Loiters
3 Earliest
4 Live
5 Genie
6 Tremor
7 Crags
13 Gruesome
16 Sandals
17 Treaty
19 Ebony
20 Prayer
22 Rider
24 Arts

10

Across
1 Pipe
4 Atishoo
8 Ignorant
9 Arc
11 Antrim
13 Engine
14 Cupid
15 Dull
17 Trot
18 Wight
20 Arctic
21 Tundra
24 Tie
25 Agnostic
26 Residue
27 Else

Down
2 Ingot
3 Exotic
4 Afar
5 Intend
6 Heavier
7 Orchestras
10 Bandmaster
12 Music
13 Eight
16 Lackeys
18 Wizard
19 Tussle
22 Dries
23 Once

11

Across
1 Chamber
5 Lane
7 Mixer
8 Jobber
10 Trek
11 Occasion
13 Layout
14 Gobble
17 Feminine
19 Pass
21 Active
22 Khaki
23 Zany
24 Leaflet

Down
1 Come to life
2 Anxiety
3 Bard
4 Reject
5 Labrador
6 Naevi
9 Underskirt
12 Quantity
15 Bradawl
16 Unreal
18 Mocha
20 Okra

12

Across
1 Eggs
3 Aspirate
9 Title
10 Isolate
11 Nip
13 Negligent
14 Centre
16 Agreed
18 Trousseau
20 Tea
22 Raisins
23 Loyal
25 Eyeteeth
26 Skew

Down
1 Eaten
2 Get
4 Stingy
5 Ironing
6 Abasement
7 Elected
8 Vein
12 Pantomime
14 Coterie
15 Respite
17 Bedsit
19 Ugly
21 Allow
24 Yak

13

Across
1 Lang
4 Wishing
8 Scornful
9 Tea
11 Artist
13 Hatred
14 Haven
15 Fame
17 Omit
18 Hoard
20 Tureen
21 Tartan
24 Hut
25 Ladybird
26 Dolphin
27 Even

Down
2 Ascot
3 Garish
4 Wife
5 Sylvan
6 Interim
7 Grandstand
10 Far-fetched
12 Talon
13 Heart
16 Marital
18 Health
19 Dabble
22 Terse
23 Eden

14

Across
1 Blazer
4 Trail
8 Frump
9 Incline
10 Epitaph
11 Puma
12 Tau
14 Peri
15 Nova
18 See
21 Luck
23 Prowler
25 Chaotic
26 Moist
27 Yield
28 Intern

Down
1 Buffet
2 Abusive
3 Emphasis
4 Tick
5 Adieu
6 Leeway
7 Tight
13 Uncommon
16 Vulpine
17 Plucky
19 Epoch
20 Cretan
22 Cease
24 Stud

15

Across
1 Tack
5 Tile
7 Insular
8 Tangling
10 Many
12 Lisp
14 Annulled
16 Sentient
17 Dale
18 Meal
19 Set-aside
22 Newborn
23 East
24 Ergo

Down
1 Tart
2 King
3 Estimate
4 Slug
5 Trembled
6 Easy
9 Abilene
11 Needled
13 Petulant
15 Notation
18 Mere
19 Sewn
20 Sane
21 Echo

16

Across

1 Grand
4 Piano
10 Debater
11 Annie
12 Riser
13 Shorten
15 Apse
17 Still
19 River
22 User
25 Dentist
27 Adder
29 Alert
30 Imitate
31 Story
32 Anger

Down

2 Rebus
3 Natural
5 Idaho
6 Nanette
7 Adore
8 Gross
9 Penny
14 Here
16 Plus
18 Tiniest
20 Iranian
21 Ideal
23 Strip
24 Greed
26 Inter
28 Drake

17

Across

1 Shopping
5 Maul
8 Figurine
9 Ecru
11 Triumvirate
14 Lug
16 Lying
17 Mat
18 Going strong
21 Tomb
22 Spitfire
24 Dark
25 Executor

Down

1 Soft
2 Ought
3 Persiflage
4 Non
6 Acclaim
7 Laureate
10 Diagnostic
12 Moist
13 Slighted
15 Glimmer
19 Guilt
20 Jeer
23 Pax

18

Across

1 Fore
5 Ming
7 Decline
8 Lovebird
10 Core
12 Jump
14 Entrance
16 Mediator
17 True
18 Stir
19 Branches
22 Succour
23 Mole
24 Evil

Down

1 Fool
2 Edge
3 Accident
4 Wild
5 Merchant
6 Give
9 Opulent
11 Recluse
13 Primrose
15 Tarragon
18 Stem
19 Back
20 Care
21 Sell

19

Across
1 Cannier
5 Seamy
8 Avers
9 Grenada
10 Propeller
12 Din
13 Untidy
14 Leaned
17 Gnu
18 Remainder
20 Embrace
21 Ionic
23 Torch
24 Annette

Down
1 Cramp
2 Née
3 Instead
4 Regale
5 Steer
6 Abandoned
7 Yearned
11 Outnumber
13 Unguent
15 Edition
16 Amoeba
18 Reach
19 Ruche
22 Nut

20

Across
1 Eaves
4 Pudding
8 Hapless
9 Order
10 Bared
11 Ominous
13 Ezra
15 Timbre
17 Geyser
20 Raid
22 Zillion
24 Indus
26 Icing
27 Leisure
28 Exerted
29 Extol

Down
1 Exhibit
2 Viper
3 Slender
4 Pastor
5 Dhoti
6 Indoors
7 Gurus
12 Magi
14 Zero
16 Malaise
18 Edifice
19 Russell
21 Angled
22 Zaire
23 Ingot
25 Doubt

21

Across
1 Deep
5 Arts
7 Respect
8 Lamp-post
10 Edam
12 Chef
14 Irritate
16 Detached
17 Dire
18 Best
19 Conclude
22 Opposer
23 Torn
24 Envy

Down
1 Deal
2 Prop
3 Astonish
4 Neat
5 Attested
6 Seem
9 Achieve
11 Altered
13 Fraction
15 Rudeness
18 Boot
19 Cope
20 Lure
21 Easy

22

Across
1 Horrors
8 Tories
9 Betting
11 Trombone
12 Rodeo
14 Anon
15 Avengers
17 Eternity
18 Hero
20 Rerun
21 Ramparts
23 Earache
24 Candle
25 Piedish

Down
2 Oberon
3 Rotten
4 Runt
5 Torment
6 Tin-opener
7 Ascension
10 Gravitate
12 Racetrack
13 Dobermans
16 Unmanly
18 Herald
19 Rushes
22 Sari

23

Across
1 Paraffin
5 Alia
8 Injuring
9 Aged
11 Hold the fort
14 Top
16 Tench
17 Moo
18 Eye-catching
21 Kiss
22 Variable
24 Rude
25 Pennines

Down
1 Pain
2 Rajah
3 For all that
4 Inn
6 Legroom
7 Addition
10 Technician
12 Tonic
13 Streaker
15 Pleased
19 Gabon
20 Zeus
23 Ale

24

Across
1 Catty
4 Pillars
8 Mordant
9 Decay
10 Onion
11 Iterate
13 Eddy
15 Tirade
17 Placid
20 Free
22 Riposte
24 Anvil
26 Acute
27 Staunch
28 Shebeen
29 Essen

Down
1 Comfort
2 Tarsi
3 Yearned
4 Putrid
5 Ladle
6 Archaic
7 Style
12 Type
14 Deft
16 Rapture
18 Leafage
19 Dolphin
21 Reason
22 Reads
23 Swede
25 Venus

25

Across

1 Pitch in
5 Whole
8 Inapt
9 Worsted
10 Toddler
11 Inner
12 Leeway
14 Beagle
17 Nadir
19 Popular
22 Languor
23 Again
24 Named
25 Theatre

Down

1 Paint
2 Twaddle
3 Hotel
4 Newark
5 Warlike
6 Often
7 Endorse
12 Lanolin
13 Aground
15 Gallant
16 Spirit
18 Denim
20 Place
21 Rinse

26

Across

7 Waiter
8 Minute
10 Proverb
11 Enrol
12 Ewer
13 Hoist
17 Quail
18 Coda
22 Waltz
23 Anthrax
24 Regard
25 Finals

Down

1 Swapped
2 Bigoted
3 Jewel
4 Finesse
5 Quirk
6 Belle
9 Abdominal
14 Buzzard
15 Journal
16 Marxist
19 Swarm
20 Elegy
21 Stain

27

Across

1 Hoarse
4 Brass
8 Arise
9 Pilsner
10 Evasion
11 Axle
12 Tie
14 Zebu
15 X-ray
18 SOS
21 Over
23 Preview
25 Massive
26 Drone
27 Leech
28 Adieus

Down

1 Heaven
2 Animate
3 Specious
4 Bold
5 Annex
6 Sorbet
7 Spent
13 Extended
16 Adipose
17 Formal
19 Spiel
20 Sweets
22 Ensue
24 Pith

28

Across

1 Spotted
5 Dick
7 Auden
8 Fascia
10 Lair
11 Bluebell
13 Upshot
14 Angler
17 Espresso
19 Sing
21 Trudge
22 Plumb
23 Flaw
24 Secrete

Down

1 Stan Laurel
2 Ordains
3 Tyne
4 Defile
5 Discerns
6 Crime
9 Clark Gable
12 Honeydew
15 Leisure
16 Assess
18 Peril
20 Epic

29

Across

1 Boot
5 Teak
7 Abusive
8 Keenness
10 Ruck
12 Fast
14 Blizzard
16 Dividend
17 Opal
18 Jerk
19 Becalmed
22 Recital
23 Pony
24 Thaw

Down

1 Bark
2 Tarn
3 Queen bee
4 Bias
5 Terrazzo
6 Kirk
9 Examine
11 Carnage
13 Trickery
15 Indicate
18 Jump
19 Beck
20 Lilt
21 Draw

30

Across

1 Eggs
4 Taught
7 Air
9 Mail
10 Idolatry
11 Vie
12 Idea
13 Dutchman
16 Materialistic
19 Assented
23 Elan
24 One
25 Bitterly
26 Rain
27 Ewe
28 Unseen
29 Dune

Down

2 Guardianship
3 Salvage
4 Tried
5 U-boat
6 Heath
8 Organisation
14 Usage
15 Chi
17 Run
18 Steered
20 Eaten
21 Terse
22 Doyen

31

Across
1 Sirens
4 Esther
7 Simpleton
9 Root
10 Lump
11 Andes
13 Bridge
14 Nurses
15 Relief
17 Carmen
19 Error
20 Site
22 Limp
23 Eagle-eyed
24 Cognac
25 Turban

Down
1 Scarab
2 Emit
3 Supine
4 Eleven
5 Tool
6 Rumpus
7 Socialite
8 Nursemaid
11 Agree
12 Sugar
15 Rustic
16 Frolic
17 Covert
18 Napkin
21 Earn
22 Leer

32

Across
1 Maid
3 Progress
9 Crypt
10 Clipper
11 Wan
13 Dalliance
14 Pariah
16 Egoist
18 Checkmate
20 Era
22 Faience
23 Pelts
25 Canberra
26 Agin

Down
1 Macaw
2 Ivy
4 Recall
5 Gaining
6 Expensive
7 Serpent
8 Stud
12 Norwegian
14 Pacific
15 Askance
17 Career
19 Expo
21 Arson
24 Log

33

Across
1 Lewes
4 Carol
10 Kidding
11 Yeast
12 Ladle
13 Instill
15 None
17 Truth
19 Atone
22 Mire
25 Cutlass
27 Racon
29 Parse
30 Eminent
31 Edith
32 Nylon

Down
2 Ended
3 Evident
5 Abyss
6 Ovation
7 Skill
8 Again
9 Stale
14 Near
16 Ohms
18 Retired
20 Terrify
21 Scope
23 Islet
24 Unite
26 Agent
28 Credo

34

Across
1 Hove
4 Insight
8 Brighton
9 Ban
11 Behind
13 Belloc
14 Eager
15 So-so
17 Undo
18 Solos
20 In vain
21 What if
24 Ire
25 Nickleby
26 Nestles
27 Says

Down
2 Oprah
3 Engine
4 Iota
5 Singer
6 Gobelin
7 Tonic sol-fa
10 Abyssinian
12 Damon
13 Below
16 Soviets
18 Signal
19 Shells
22 Tabby
23 Acts

35

Across
1 Knickers
5 Hear
8 Legation
9 Fuss
11 Transaction
14 Rag
16 Dream
17 Gun
18 Predicament
21 Rake
22 Scribble
24 Dane
25 Stagnant

Down
1 Kilt
2 Ingot
3 Kith and kin
4 Roo
6 Exuding
7 Resonant
10 Scampering
12 Sheba
13 Prepared
15 Gherkin
19 Tibia
20 Vent
23 Cut

36

Across
1 Thin
5 King
7 Opinion
8 Stretchy
10 Cage
12 Smug
14 Platinum
16 Severest
17 Game
18 Stun
19 Connects
22 Elevate
23 Rely
24 Need

Down
1 Toss
2 Note
3 Disciple
4 Tiny
5 Knocking
6 Gaze
9 Tempest
11 Gourmet
13 Guernsey
15 Antennae
18 Spar
19 Chef
20 Even
21 Sped

37

Across
1 Bowline
8 Galley
9 Stealth
11 Sediment
12 Piety
14 Undo
15 Soya bean
17 Cocktail
18 Cede
20 Error
21 Antidote
23 Sadness
24 Eloper
25 Algebra

Down
2 Obtain
3 Lean-to
4 Nuts
5 Habitat
6 Blue Peter
7 Bystander
10 Hedonists
12 Purchaser
13 Education
16 Studies
18 Cringe
19 Dowser
22 Earl

38

Across
1 Braised
5 Leaks
8 Optic
9 Ravioli
10 Hotheaded
12 Oil
13 Papaya
14 Addict
17 Row
18 Forcemeat
20 Omicron
21 Aesop
23 Sweat
24 Ordered

Down
1 Broth
2 Act
3 Society
4 Deride
5 Livid
6 Apologise
7 Skillet
11 Typewrite
13 Parlous
15 Die-hard
16 Franco
18 First
19 Tepid
22 Sir

39

Across
1 Laager
4 Louts
8 Aster
9 Measure
10 Senegal
11 Byre
12 Lop
14 Gain
15 Rows
18 Goa
21 Abba
23 Devizes
25 Stirrup
26 Ounce
27 Cream
28 Asides

Down
1 Liaise
2 Antenna
3 Enraging
4 Liar
5 Usury
6 Shekel
7 Small
13 Previous
16 Wizened
17 Parsec
19 Adept
20 Ushers
22 Bride
24 Trim

40

Across
1 Lifer
4 Islay
10 Apparel
11 Allot
12 False
13 Freeway
15 Safe
17 Petty
19 Study
22 Efta
25 Despise
27 No way
29 Twang
30 Caravan
31 Neath
32 Omens

Down
2 Impel
3 Earnest
5 Scare
6 Allowed
7 Gaffe
8 Cliff
9 Stays
14 Rest
16 Ayes
18 Enslave
20 Tantrum
21 Edits
23 Fence
24 Hyena
26 Ingot
28 Woven

41

Across
1 Sleeping
7 Booty
8 Outrigger
9 Era
10 Pond
11 Closer
13 Gasper
14 Slopes
17 Setter
18 Snow
20 Sip
22 Leviathan
23 Loose
24 Preserve

Down
1 Stoop
2 Extends
3 Prim
4 Niggle
5 Rover
6 Tyrants
7 Bristle
12 Textile
13 Ghostly
15 Panther
16 Denver
17 Spool
19 Wince
21 Lass

42

Across
1 Alley
2 Barber
9 Screams
10 Tramp
11 Soda
12 Indiana
13 Tic
14 Isle
16 Thou
18 Ore
20 Aerates
21 Elba
24 Pilau
25 Avoided
26 Tested
27 Green

Down
1 Assist
2 Lurid
3 Year
5 Antidote
6 Bravado
7 Repeat
8 Aspic
13 Test-tube
15 Strolls
17 Carpet
18 Oscar
19 Warden
22 Ledge
23 Long

43

Across
1 Gnus
4 Papers
7 Eke
9 Twit
10 Ascended
11 Far
12 Gala
13 Luncheon
16 Approximately
19 Chuckled
23 Arch
24 Raw
25 Brochure
26 Lair
27 Axe
28 Lawyer
29 Rung

Down
2 New Hampshire
3 Set fair
4 Pearl
5 Pecan
6 Ranch
8 Recollection
14 Unite
15 Cha
17 Oak
18 Trawler
20 Cocoa
21 Lousy
22 Drear

44

Across
1 Collie
4 Shuns
8 Learn
9 Peasant
10 Enlarge
11 Rear
12 Due
14 Stun
15 Nous
18 Toy
21 Tome
23 Ovation
25 Patient
26 Guise
27 Dirge
28 Ardent

Down
1 Called
2 Leaflet
3 Ignorant
4 Stay
5 Usage
6 Saturn
7 Speed
13 Endanger
16 Utilise
17 Stupid
19 Youth
20 Unrest
22 Motor
24 Mere

45

Across
1 Miner
4 Profits
8 Abreast
9 Deter
10 Dwelt
11 Oarsmen
13 Oils
15 Record
17 Tousle
20 Epic
22 Cherish
24 Upset
26 Alive
27 Epicure
28 Lithium
29 Tract

Down
1 Meander
2 Nurse
3 Reactor
4 Petrol
5 Order
6 Isthmus
7 Siren
12 Asti
14 Ides
16 Chemist
18 Oculist
19 Entreat
21 Phlegm
22 Crawl
23 Iceni
25 Sauna

46

Across
1 Blankets
7 Titch
8 Ambulance
9 Rub
10 Dome
11 Beirut
13 Fungus
14 Tiffin
17 Agadir
18 Anti
20 Lit
22 Legionary
23 Chime
24 Arboreal

Down
1 Bland
2 Albumen
3 Kill
4 Tender
5 Start
6 Shebeen
7 Terrain
12 Durable
13 Fallacy
15 Fanfare
16 Linger
17 Attic
19 Idyll
21 Hobo

47

Across
1 Polly
4 Titian
9 Natural
10 Total
11 Ions
12 Penguin
13 Dis
14 Tutu
16 Even
18 Aim
20 Omnibus
21 Apse
24 Eyrie
25 Exploit
26 Spells
27 Noose

Down
1 Pencil
2 Latin
3 Yard
5 In tandem
6 Intrude
7 & 17 Nolens volens
8 Slaps
13 Dumb-bell
15 Unnerve
17 See 7
18 Aster
19 Fettle
22 Photo
23 Spin

48

Across
1 Genie
4 Allergy
8 Aladdin
9 Movie
10 Stair
11 Insured
13 Epée
15 Dressy
17 Creeds
20 Rake
22 Cabinet
24 Voter
26 Aping
27 Lillian
28 Trestle
29 Sheds

Down
1 Grassed
2 Nyasa
3 Endures
4 Auntie
5 Lambs
6 Reverse
7 Yield
12 Neck
14 Pyre
16 Ebbtide
18 Revolts
19 Springs
21 Attlee
22 Chart
23 Night
25 Trite

49

Across

4 Picker
5 Door
7 Parlour
10 Stagy
11 Pipette
12 Entry
14 Assured
15 Prank
16 Girdles
20 Stern
21 Sirloin
22 Colt
23 Claret

Down

1 Scalp
2 Set up
3 Portend
4 Peal
6 Regard
8 Oilskin
9 Refunds
10 Steeper
13 Erotic
14 Angrily
17 Lisle
18 Slurp
19 Sift

50

Across

1 Foreign
5 Sick
7 Radio
8 Therms
10 Edam
11 Contract
13 Catnap
14 Decade
17 Practise
19 Bang
21 Search
22 Smash
23 Idol
24 Written

Down

1 Fire escape
2 Radiant
3 Iron
4 Notion
5 Spectres
6 Comma
9 Strengthen
12 Pastoral
15 Adamant
16 Eschew
18 Ahead
20 Asti

51

Across

1 Proper
2 Gating
7 Abhorrent
9 Emus
10 Erne
11 Beast
13 States
14 Heyday
15 Aliens
17 Apathy
19 Stilt
20 Shut
22 Polo
23 Sacristan
24 Relish
25 Airmen

Down

1 Pliers
2 Pubs
3 Rhodes
4 Garish
5 Tune
6 Gaiety
7 Audacious
8 Tradition
11 Beans
12 Tempt
15 Answer
16 Starch
17 Alaska
18 Yeoman
21 Taxi
22 Pair

52

Across
1 Cauls
4 Forth
10 Spencer
11 Largo
12 Laden
13 Captive
15 Scar
17 Cameo
19 Idaho
22 Dodo
25 Painter
27 Sober
29 Cabot
30 Asinine
31 Beret
32 Crisp

Down
2 Amend
3 License
5 Oxlip
6 Tarnish
7 Psalm
8 Erica
9 Coven
14 Arid
16 Code
18 Amiable
20 Dossier
21 Space
23 Organ
24 Cruet
26 Title
28 Bliss

53

Across
1 Mission
5 Aries
8 NALGO
9 Tristan
10 Harbour
11 Ozone
12 Breach
14 Recess
17 Resin
19 Pluvial
22 Algeria
23 Treat
24 Errol
25 Scratch

Down
1 Mynah
2 Splurge
3 Iroko
4 Nature
5 Adipose
6 Intro
7 Singers
12 Barrage
13 Central
15 Evident
16 Speaks
18 Sugar
20 Utter
21 Latch

54

Across
1 Talk
4 Turkey
7 Ava
9 Stir
10 Chinaman
11 Ali
12 Alec
13 Test-tube
16 Mediterranean
19 By the bye
23 Nude
24 Los
25 Parlance
26 Trod
27 Goo
28 Polony
29 Pony

Down
2 Artilleryman
3 Karachi
4 Tacit
5 Rails
6 Exact
8 Darby and Joan
14 Early
15 Tea
17 Tee
18 Non-stop
20 Hello
21 Bingo
22 Elegy

55

Across
1 Unrest
7 Reigned
8 Minister
9 Snare
10 Vigil
11 Iced
12 Ratty
15 Table
16 Glebe
19 Axel
20 Bathe
21 Frost
22 Ethereal
23 Analogy
24 Chaser

Down
1 Unmoving
2 Renegade
3 Sisal
4 Per
5 Agenda
6 Regret
7 Reliability
9 Sere
13 Tactless
14 Yodeller
15 Text
17 Larynx
18 Basalt
20 Beech
22 Egg

56

Across
1 Ferry
4 Tails
10 Autopsy
11 Borne
12 Cargo
13 Letters
15 Over
17 Chafe
19 Sense
22 Need
25 Cascade
27 Union
29 Fling
30 Imagine
31 Rebel
32 Verge

Down
2 Enter
3 Reproof
5 Abbot
6 Largess
7 Farce
8 Cycle
9 Feast
14 Erse
16 Vend
18 Hostile
20 Educate
21 Scoff
23 Eerie
24 Under
26 Angle
28 Icing

57

Across
1 Hyde
3 Rollicks
9 Rider
10 Tangent
11 Elk
13 Thesaurus
14 Ranger
16 Keenly
18 Fragrance
20 Ear
22 Elopers
23 Divan
25 Hesitant
26 Sway

Down
1 Horde
2 Dud
4 Outset
5 Lineage
6 Clearance
7 Satisfy
8 Writ
12 Kangaroos
14 Refresh
15 Earnest
17 Unison
19 Ends
21 Rangy
24 Vow

58

Across

1 Concert
5 Hauls
8 Venus
9 Scruffy
10 Relieve
11 Outdo
12 Tussle
14 Anorak
17 Avert
19 Antique
22 Nuptial
23 Twist
24 Ellen
25 Dilemma

Down

1 Cover
2 Nonplus
3 Ensue
4 Tester
5 Harpoon
6 Unfit
7 Shylock
12 Trainee
13 Latvian
15 Requiem
16 Failed
18 Expel
20 Total
21 Extra

59

Across

1 Firmer
4 Meant
8 Copes
9 Babylon
10 Lessens
11 Twee
12 Ham
14 Veil
15 Urge
18 Yap
21 Able
23 Raccoon
25 Sandals
26 Kendo
27 Loyal
28 Unison

Down

1 Facile
2 Riposte
3 Easterly
4 Moby
5 Allow
6 Tender
7 Abash
13 Munchkin
16 Grounds
17 Vassal
19 Press
20 Inborn
22 Lanky
24 Ball

60

Across

7 Rubber
8 Czechs
10 Fellini
11 Lotto
12 Rare
13 Debar
17 Teddy
18 Gave
22 Windy
23 Weather
24 Capers
25 Matron

Down

1 Prefers
2 Abelard
3 Begin
4 Azaleas
5 Acute
6 Ascot
9 Eiderdown
14 New York
15 Fathers
16 Jeering
19 Twice
20 Snipe
21 Japan

61

Across
1 Pencil
4 Vanya
8 Quail
9 Beehive
10 Enigmas
11 Menu
12 Ebb
14 Ogen
15 Asia
18 Eat
21 Echo
23 Request
25 Oblique
26 Elude
27 Aloha
28 Ascent

Down
1 Piquet
2 Nearing
3 Illumine
4 View
5 Naive
6 Avenue
7 Abuse
13 Banquets
16 Ice cube
17 Pelota
19 Tried
20 Street
22 Hello
24 Aqua

62

Across
1 Chain
4 Jehovah
8 Transit
9 Lochs
10 Andre
11 Awesome
13 Gage
15 Sludge
17 Fresco
20 Oath
22 Commune
24 Uncut
26 Banjo
27 Abalone
28 Layette
29 Banal

Down
1 Cutlass
2 Award
3 Nest egg
4 Jet lag
5 Halve
6 Vacuous
7 Haste
12 Weft
14 Aeon
16 Unmanly
18 Rhubarb
19 Oatmeal
21 Aerate
22 Cabal
23 U-boat
25 Clown

63

Across
1 Paltry
7 Farmers
8 Sheraton
9 Catty
10 Piety
11 Boor
12 Stalk
15 Shaky
16 Tense
19 Mesa
20 Forgo
21 Flair
22 Accolade
23 Enthuse
24 Mettle

Down
1 Passport
2 Liegeman
3 Ready
4 Pan
5 Impart
6 Brutal
7 Forbearance
9 Cosy
13 Aberrant
14 Kerosene
15 Seer
17 Ealing
18 Smithy
20 Froze
22 Asp

64

Across

1 Brighton
7 Early
8 Grenadier
9 Ida
10 Note
11 Mussel
13 Rhymes
14 Porous
17 Gorgon
18 Mesh
20 Rye
22 Fruitless
23 Assay
24 Vendetta

Down

1 Begin
2 Ineptly
3 Heal
4 Odious
5 Frail
6 Gyrates
7 Erosion
12 Terrify
13 Retreat
15 Overeat
16 Module
17 Gesso
19 Hosea
21 Stud

65

Across

1 Meet
4 Eeyore
7 Ira
9 Spit
10 Rasputin
11 All
12 Grin
13 Yielding
16 Ambassadorial
19 Internet
23 Sage
24 Hop
25 Waterloo
26 Oval
27 Run
28 Cannon
29 Deed

Down

2 Experimental
3 Titania
4 Early
5 Yes we
6 Round
8 Sign language
14 Image
15 Leo
17 Sir
18 Respond
20 Elena
21 Nylon
22 Thorn

66

Across

1 Oaring
7 Spiring
8 Excavate
9 Qatar
10 Hotel
11 Maul
12 Askew
15 Tacky
16 Lager
19 Nova
20 Fibre
21 Joist
22 Wharfage
23 Geordie
24 Rhodes

Down

1 Overhaul
2 Reciting
3 Navel
4 Ape
5 Trials
6 Intake
7 Stomachache
9 Quay
13 Keyboard
14 Wireless
15 Trot
17 Azores
18 Ensure
20 Forth
22 Wig

67

Across

1 Sound
4 Bight
10 Incense
11 Eight
12 Egret
13 Entraps
15 Okra
17 Okapi
19 Fight
22 Daft
25 Eclipse
27 Anger
29 Cajun
30 Ominous
31 My way
32 Anise

Down

2 Occur
3 Non-stop
5 Inert
6 Hogwash
7 Fiver
8 Fever
9 Stash
14 Naff
16 Kids
18 Killjoy
20 Italian
21 Deuce
23 Aesop
24 Brass
26 Panda
28 Gross

68

Across

1 Morpheus
7 Elves
8 Middlesex
9 III
10 Crew
11 Patrol
13 Result
14 Access
17 Status
18 Form
20 Act
22 Afternoon
23 Tonic
24 Amethyst

Down

1 Mimic
2 Redress
3 Hold
4 Unseat
5 Avail
6 Useless
7 Extract
12 Almanac
13 Regatta
15 Economy
16 Custom
17 Stink
19 Monet
21 Fret

69

Across

1 Farther
8 Figure
9 Norwich
11 Hampered
12 Snare
14 Eddy
15 Narrator
17 Theology
18 Avon
20 Alert
21 Massenet
23 Defunct
24 Notice
25 Fleeced

Down

2 Abound
3 Tawdry
4 Each
5 Disport
6 Lucrative
7 Deodorant
10 Harangued
12 Sentiment
13 Adversity
16 Fluency
18 Allure
19 Oracle
22 Teal

70

Across
1 Eaten
4 Choler
9 Brummel
10 Lotus
11 Rake
12 Natural
13 Gig
14 Thee
16 Rill
18 Elm
20 Limpets
21 Epic
24 Verso
25 Endowed
26 Remiss
27 Nasty

Down
1 Embark
2 Truck
3 Name
5 Half-term
6 Lateral
7 Rustle
8 Slang
13 Generous
15 Humdrum
17 Plover
18 Esher
19 Acidly
22 Powys
23 Odin

71

Across
1 Surgeon
5 Baba
7 Ollie
8 Knight
10 Keen
11 Sentence
13 Issued
14 Teapot
17 Emphasis
19 Main
21 Murder
22 Tutti
23 Mesh
24 Lyrical

Down
1 Stockpiles
2 Rollers
3 Ever
4 Nikkei
5 Bristles
6 Behan
9 Centennial
12 Verandah
15 Plastic
16 Wirral
18 Pause
20 Star

72

Across
1 Webb
4 Sights
7 Row
9 Stoa
10 Alarming
11 War
12 Anil
13 Drearier
16 Quadruplicate
19 Assemble
23 Rage
24 Lee
25 Separate
26 Fate
27 Gnu
28 Jersey
29 Lurk

Down
2 Extinguished
3 Brawled
4 Sward
5 Graze
6 Tamar
8 Investigator
14 Repel
15 Ali
17 Ram
18 Careful
20 Evade
21 Brass
22 Elegy

73

Across
1 Court
4 Alight
9 Toddler
10 Gorge
11 Lark
12 Blatant
13 SOS
14 Grit
16 Deep
18 Gas
20 Resolve
21 Over
24 Agent
25 Reserve
26 Nation
27 Dwell

Down
1 Cattle
2 Under
3 Tall
5 Laggards
6 Garbage
7 Twenty
8 Grabs
13 Stiletto
15 Respect
17 Ordain
18 Genre
19 Ordeal
22 Verse
23 Used

74

Across
1 Guard
4 Density
8 Admiral
9 Lined
10 Hindi
11 General
13 Need
15 Craggy
17 Geisha
20 Over
22 Climate
24 Rumba
26 Arena
27 Titlark
28 Potency
29 Cairn

Down
1 Graphic
2 Amman
3 Darling
4 Deluge
5 Nylon
6 Innards
7 Yodel
12 Edge
14 Eyot
16 Aliment
18 Erratic
19 Alaskan
21 Vestry
22 Clasp
23 Again
25 Miami

75

Across
1 Loan
4 Parents
8 Commerce
9 Vim
11 Ludlow
13 Petrol
14 Dated
15 Tube
17 Knur
18 Wench
20 Onager
21 Hermit
24 Ova
25 Libretto
26 Satchel
27 Ache

Down
2 Ovoid
3 Nimrod
4 Perk
5 Reeked
6 Navarin
7 Similarity
10 Gluttonous
12 Waver
13 Perch
16 Blatant
18 Wealth
19 Hedera
22 Match
23 Obol

76

Across

1 Broaden
5 Arrow
8 Eider
9 Unarmed
10 Streatham
12 Nil
13 Greets
14 Mossad
17 Rio
18 Recumbent
20 Legible
21 Sorry
23 Agnes
24 Easiest

Down

1 Bless
2 Old
3 Dormant
4 Naught
5 Alarm
6 Reminisce
7 Waddled
11 Reed-organ
13 Gorilla
15 Osmosis
16 Accede
18 Robes
19 Tryst
22 Roe

77

Across

1 Diss
4 Jockey
7 UFO
9 Oder
10 Kindlier
11 Gee
12 Isle
13 Scotties
16 Dinner jackets
19 Accident
23 So-so
24 Aft
25 Flunkeys
26 Roar
27 Toe
28 Writhe
29 Lads

Down

2 Indistinctly
3 Surgeon
4 Jokes
5 Congo
6 Eilat
8 Desert island
14 Cajun
15 Tic
17 End
18 Kestrel
20 Inner
21 Exeat
22 Taste

78

Across

1 Special
5 Offa
7 Fauna
8 Greeks
10 Iota
11 Wanderer
13 Indent
14 Unseen
17 Nazareth
19 Gulf
21 Oblige
22 Index
23 Many
24 Kindred

Down

1 Sufficient
2 Equated
3 Ivan
4 Log-jam
5 Overdone
6 Fakir
9 Transfixed
12 Enormity
15 Ecuador
16 Streak
18 Zebra
20 Lion

79

Across
- **1** Canter
- **4** Berry
- **8** Unite
- **9** Admiral
- **10** Blemish
- **11** Blue
- **12** Ear
- **14** Mesh
- **15** Echo
- **18** Tie
- **21** Carp
- **23** Artisan
- **25** Leveret
- **26** Raise
- **27** Stray
- **28** Oddest

Down
- **1** Chubby
- **2** Naivete
- **3** Eyesight
- **4** Bump
- **5** Rural
- **6** Yelled
- **7** Lathe
- **13** Restored
- **16** Hostile
- **17** Scales
- **19** Earth
- **20** Unrest
- **22** River
- **24** Army

80

Across
- **1** Pitch in
- **5** Towed
- **8** Throb
- **9** Painter
- **10** Heartless
- **12** Hen
- **13** Estate
- **14** Ignore
- **17** Hip
- **18** Knowledge
- **20** Besides
- **21** Amble
- **23** Tools
- **24** Lottery

Down
- **1** Patch
- **2** Tar
- **3** Habitat
- **4** Nephew
- **5** Tails
- **6** Watchword
- **7** Derange
- **11** Antipasto
- **13** Exhibit
- **15** Gallant
- **16** Morsel
- **18** Kudos
- **19** Enemy
- **22** Bee

81

Across
- **1** Knocker
- **5** Bout
- **7** Taste
- **8** Snooze
- **10** Lark
- **11** Multiple
- **13** Deejay
- **14** Instep
- **17** Untangle
- **19** Oxen
- **21** Circle
- **22** Harem
- **23** Fact
- **24** Sunbeam

Down
- **1** Kettledrum
- **2** Observe
- **3** Knew
- **4** Risqué
- **5** Boosting
- **6** Unzip
- **9** Keeping mum
- **12** Wainscot
- **15** Tax-free
- **16** Pliers
- **18** Taiga
- **20** Shun

82

Across

7 Trains
8 Potter
10 Avarice
11 Dirge
12 Gale
13 Order
17 Large
18 Dear
22 About
23 Traffic
24 Romany
25 Fracas

Down

1 Strange
2 Capable
3 Unfit
4 Soldier
5 Store
6 Brief
9 Segregate
14 Lasting
15 Perfect
16 Precise
19 Tarry
20 Comma
21 Marry

83

Across

1 Weigh
4 Kingcup
8 Stagger
9 Salvo
10 Allow
11 Thyroid
13 Area
15 Embryo
17 Loosen
20 Soft
22 Holster
24 Habit
26 Lunge
27 Collier
28 Theatre
29 Offal

Down

1 Wastage
2 In all
3 Highway
4 Karate
5 Nasty
6 Callous
7 Proud
12 Half
14 Rose
16 Balance
18 Othello
19 Natural
21 Oracle
22 Holst
23 Treat
25 Brief

84

Across

1 Even
5 Tied
7 Ukulele
8 Strength
10 Toby
12 Fits
14 Legation
16 Follower
17 Rate
18 Fist
19 Bookworm
22 Rubella
23 Tray
24 Dime

Down

1 Eros
2 Nude
3 Bungalow
4 Seth
5 Testator
6 Deny
9 Tripoli
11 Bloater
13 Salutary
15 Gargoyle
18 Fiat
19 Baby
20 Woad
21 Mire

85

Across
4 Picker
5 Lily
7 Scandal
10 Steep
11 Tyranny
12 Erode
14 Banshee
15 Magus
16 Steered
20 Tatty
21 Susanna
22 Dire
23 States

Down
1 Scant
2 Debar
3 Kintyre
4 Pace
6 Yields
8 Dynasty
9 Lassoes
10 Sneezes
13 Hazard
14 Bustard
17 Rusty
18 Darts
19 Onus

86

Across
1 Bangers
8 Enmesh
9 Usurper
11 Sherlock
12 Ceded
14 Anon
15 Composed
17 Moriarty
18 Slow
20 Stern
21 Literate
23 Spooned
24 Tipped
25 Bengali

Down
2 Austen
3 Garden
4 Rues
5 Entraps
6 Lemon-sole
7 Shakedown
10 Rheostats
12 Carmelite
13 Doorsteps
16 Parries
18 Strong
19 Orwell
22 Epée

87

Across
1 Thorough
5 Fair
8 Inciting
9 Pomp
11 Reformatory
14 Alb
16 Twine
17 Sin
18 Judiciously
21 Roué
22 Schooled
24 Mink
25 Quatrain

Down
1 Toil
2 Oscar
3 Out of stock
4 Gin
6 Amorous
7 Replying
10 Waterspout
12 Rhino
13 Marjoram
15 Bedouin
19 Yalta
20 Odin
23 Cru

88

Across
1 Sweeter
5 Sunny
8 Agent
9 Precise
10 Trainee
11 Ahead
12 Futile
14 Demand
17 Icing
19 Objects
22 Attract
23 Alien
24 Eerie
25 Essence

Down
1 Start
2 Elegant
3 Titan
4 Rapier
5 Seepage
6 Naïve
7 Yielded
12 Frigate
13 Luggage
15 Auction
16 Bottle
18 Inter
20 Jeans
21 Singe

89

Across
1 Salve
4 Tsunami
8 Terrier
9 Sauna
10 Hedge
11 Actuary
13 Note
15 Length
17 Decent
20 Item
22 Warrior
24 Elgin
26 Rouse
27 Unaware
28 Stealth
29 Ditty

Down
1 Satchel
2 Lurid
3 Evident
4 Threat
5 Upset
6 Adulate
7 Italy
12 Cede
14 Ohio
16 Nurture
18 Emerald
19 Tensely
21 Trough
22 Works
23 Ideal
25 Giant

90

Across
1 Sear
4 Sucker
7 Act
9 Guam
10 Anarchic
11 Air
12 Ovid
13 Entreaty
16 Scandalmonger
19 Standing
23 Test
24 You
25 Soft-soap
26 Reel
27 Sea
28 Classy
29 Lint

Down
2 Equivocation
3 Ramadan
4 Stare
5 Craft
6 Emcee
8 Wittgenstein
14 Nylon
15 Rho
17 Dud
18 Natural
20 Natal
21 Icons
22 Gypsy

91

Across

1 Trees
4 Urging
9 Riposte
10 Arson
11 Ally
12 Athlete
13 Pal
14 Scar
16 Gets
18 ATS
20 Amassed
21 Stir
24 Hindi
25 Lateral
26 & 27 Walter Mitty

Down

1 Tartan
2 Expel
3 So-so
5 Roadhogs
6 Inspect
7 Gannet
8 Metal
13 Pristine
15 Channel
17 Cashew
18 Adult
19 Frilly
22 Tarot
23 Item

92

Across

1 Hamster
5 Damn
7 & 8 India rubber
10 Cole
11 Florists
13 Tested
14 Tender
17 European
19 Scan
21 Stoned
22 Forum
23 Eyes
24 Grammar

Down

1 Haircutter
2 Meddles
3 Teak
4 Rarely
5 Debarred
6 Meets
9 Astronomer
12 Helpings
15 Decorum
16 Lapdog
18 Ratty
20 Offa

93

Across

1 Boulder
8 No-ball
9 Lynched
11 Deployed
12 Refer
14 Oner
15 Diaspora
17 Globulin
18 Veto
20 Miser
21 Chilling
23 Thawing
24 Stuffy
25 Defrost

Down

2 Oxygen
3 Locker
4 Eyed
5 Jobless
6 Lazybones
7 Gladiator
10 Deficient
12 Roughcast
13 Ferocious
16 Qualify
18 Viewer
19 Tennis
22 Ghee

94

Across
1 Right
4 Align
10 Reserve
11 Delve
12 Obese
13 Contact
15 Styx
17 Write
19 Earth
22 Aunt
25 Western
27 Trait
29 Ended
30 Teacher
31 Weary
32 Story

Down
2 Issue
3 Hardest
5 Laden
6 Gallant
7 Brook
8 Mercy
9 Heath
14 Oxen
16 Tear
18 Residue
20 Attract
21 Owner
23 Unity
24 Start
26 Elder
28 Abhor

95

Across
1 Caulks
4 Cruise
7 Hermitage
9 Seek
10 Etui
11 Regal
13 Supper
14 Plaque
15 Cherub
17 Embers
19 Sepia
20 Moth
22 Step
23 Oenophile
24 Scarce
25 Simmer

Down
1 Census
2 Leek
3 Simper
4 Catnap
5 Urge
6 Excite
7 Hey-presto
8 Etiquette
11 Remus
12 Llama
15 Campus
16 Before
17 Eights
18 Sapper
21 Hear
22 Slim

96

Across
1 Schnapps
5 Shot
8 Inviting
9 Cram
11 Radiologist
14 Cow
16 Delhi
17 Yen
18 Francophile
21 Orgy
22 Attorney
24 Deem
25 Pristine

Down
1 Skit
2 Haver
3 Autodidact
4 Pun
6 Horrify
7 Tempting
10 Solicitous
12 Oxlip
13 Scaffold
15 Wrangle
19 Ennui
20 Byre
23 Tar

97

Across
1 Awry
5 Toff
7 Enslave
8 Galleons
10 Maul
12 Ovid
14 Infinite
16 Snowshoe
17 Sore
18 Reef
19 Set aside
22 Learned
23 Seal
24 Erin

Down
1 Agog
2 Yell
3 Astonish
4 Mars
5 Terminus
6 Feel
9 Advance
11 Uttered
13 Downfall
15 Fretting
18 Rows
19 Spar
20 Side
21 Earn

98

Across
1 Djinn
4 Rummy
10 Tenpins
11 Whist
12 Gusto
13 Nodding
15 Magi
17 Seven
19 Large
22 Toys
25 Soldier
27 Sheba
29 Onset
30 Already
31 Usury
32 Ashes

Down
1 Jones
3 Noisome
5 Unwed
6 Mailing
7 Stags
8 Using
9 Stage
14 Oily
16 Ante
18 Enlists
20 Asserts
21 Aston
23 Organ
24 Satyr
26 Inter
28 Erase

99

Across
4 Bigger
5 Mist
7 Camphor
10 Melon
11 Towered
12 Rival
14 Divulge
15 Topaz
16 Sousing
20 Foehn
21 Tagalog
22 Rank
23 Object

Down
1 Egypt
2 Below
3 Sine die
4 Bray
6 Thorax
8 Horizon
9 Request
10 Merging
13 Colour
14 Dashing
17 Iambi
18 Gavel
19 Jolt

100

Across
1 Penned
4 Dragon
7 Sweetener
9 Eros
10 Lone
11 Amber
13 Thirst
14 Dinghy
15 Boiled
17 Seance
19 Women
20 Riot
22 Scum
23 Reykjavik
24 Hawker
25 Energy

Down
1 Patent
2 News
3 Dreamt
4 Deemed
5 Abel
6 Nicety
7 Solicitor
8 Roughneck
11 Askew
12 Ripen
15 Borsch
16 Docker
17 Senate
18 Enmity
21 Teak
22 Side

101

Across
1 Purr
5 Mitt
7 Ingrate
8 Kneecaps
10 Neat
12 Hasp
14 Increase
16 Hellenic
17 Spit
18 Star
19 Mattress
22 Origins
23 Noon
24 Tarn

Down
1 Pink
2 Rile
3 Agrarian
4 Pass
5 Meanders
6 Tilt
9 Nearest
11 Assails
13 Poltroon
15 Cocktail
18 Sign
19 Mail
20 Rest
21 Soon

102

Across
1 Emcee
4 Squared
8 Quavers
9 Given
10 Imari
11 Endured
13 Name
15 Energy
17 Riddle
20 Eton
22 Shiatsu
24 Tarot
26 Evens
27 Vanilla
28 Letters
29 Egypt

Down
1 Enquire
2 Clara
3 Evening
4 System
5 Urged
6 Revered
7 Dined
12 Nero
14 Ayes
16 Eminent
18 Intense
19 Extract
21 Turves
22 Smell
23 Taste
25 Rally

103

Across
1 Gift
4 Trapped
8 Zimbabwe
9 Run
11 Let out
13 Quince
14 Revue
15 Cove
17 Grow
18 Harsh
20 Donjon
21 Temper
24 Tun
25 Dabbling
26 Derange
27 Hock

Down
2 Idiot
3 Tabour
4 Tuba
5 Avenue
6 Partner
7 Donkey-work
10 Elucidated
12 Texan
13 Quest
16 Ventnor
18 Hoyden
19 Health
22 Panic
23 Oboe

104

Across
1 Chuckle
5 Eight
8 Dress
9 Leaning
10 Restraint
12 See
13 Portly
14 Famous
17 Eft
18 Silliness
20 Engrave
21 Horde
23 Tempt
24 Eastern

Down
1 Cider
2 Use
3 Kestrel
4 Eclair
5 Exact
6 Gritstone
7 Tigress
11 Stratagem
13 Present
15 Alights
16 Allege
18 Start
19 Stern
22 Rye

www.ingramcontent.com/pod-product-compliance
Ingram Content Group UK Ltd.
Pitfield, Milton Keynes, MK11 3LW, UK
UKHW040639280225
455688UK00002B/19